Australia:

Boom to Bust

The Great Australian Credit and Property Bubble

Lindsay David

Introduction   4

Australia: The Lucky Country?:   7

Apples and Oranges: 13

Ignorance, Familiarity and Misinformation: 24

The First Pillar: Financial Institutions: 37

China: The Bubble to End All Bubbles: 59

The Second Pillar: Natural Resources: 72

The Third Pillar: Real Estate: 91

Politicians and Reserve Bankers: Where did they go wrong?:   125

The International Event that Causes a Domino Effect: 144

The Domestic Event that Causes the Knockout of Pillars One and Three: 172

How Bad Does it Get?:   195

Conclusion: 208

Introduction

After spending the last nine years in Europe working and living through the most challenging financial crisis in recent memory, I permanently returned to my native Australia. I'd left Sydney in late 2004. At that point in time, Australia was a fundamentally strong country. The cost of living, although slightly on the high side, seemed manageable for the ordinary Australian. The mining industry was growing at a fast pace, and property costs were very expensive relative to household incomes. I lived in Lausanne, Switzerland, from 2004 until 2010, and spent the remainder of my nine-year tenure in the Central London neighborhood of St John's Wood. My time in Europe was challenging with modest success as a strategy and business development consultant, and, more recently, I cofounded the startup clean technology company GreenRigCo, which is based in Houston, Texas.

In 2013, I was the second-youngest student in IMD's Executive MBA program. It was the most challenging year of my life. Between starting up a clean technology company based in the United States, and attending the world's most challenging and stimulating Executive MBA program based in Switzerland—all while living in London—I was relieved when I received my MBA certificate. On the first day of the program, Phil Rozensweig, our strategy professor and program director, told us, "On November 15th, 2013, you will get your life back. Until then you will not have much of a life." He was right.

The students were given very challenging assignments and consulting projects related to strategy, leadership, organizational design, foreign direct investment, customer learning experiences and human resources. We were also given two very challenging finance-related assignments. As most of my fellow students were high-ranking executives within large multinational organizations, they were able to undertake the finance assignments and hone in on the financials of the company they work for. My clean technology company was brand new and too small to have adequate data to undertake the critical components of the assignment. My finance professor, Salvatore Cantale, advised me to base the two finance assignments on a large and complex multinational corporation. As an Australian, and based on my frequent business trips to China and years spent researching the Chinese economy and its impact on Australia, I chose the company Rio Tinto for this purpose. Although the common view is that Australia will always benefit from continuous Chinese prosperity, my gut was telling me otherwise.

Through my research, I uncovered so many macroeconomic factors and challenges that could affect the financial health of Rio Tinto that I began to dive deeper and do research on a greater scale, investigating what my gut had always suspected. I was diving into what I knew would uncover incredible findings. Australia is living in a bubble. It's at the tail end of the beginning of what could be an unavoidable catastrophic economic downturn.

This book lays a foundation describing why the Australian economy is simply not prepared for an economic downturn.

I had left Australia in 2004, at a time when Australia's Gross Domestic Product was $859 billion. In December of 2013, I returned home to a $1.52 trillion economy. I had traveled back to Australia regularly for short visits over the previous nine years. Returning every few months for short stays, I saw what I believed to be large incremental rises in the cost of living for Australians. When I arrived back in Australia with a wife and ambitions to start a family, I was astonished at what I saw. After nine years spent living in European cities famous for their high costs of living, it was shocking to see how expensive it was to live by the southern beaches of Sydney, and in Sydney in general. However, when you start to investigate the root causes of why Australia has become such an expensive place to live, it all becomes very simple to understand. When it comes to economics, Australia has made the big mistake of believing its economy is "different," and that it will only grow. Unfortunately, history has an excellent track record of proving wrong any country that attempts to defy the common laws of economics.

Chapter One

Australia: The Lucky Country?

Before I begin what may seem to be a very critical analysis of the Australian economy, I first want to say that Australia is truly an incredible country. I'm proud to be an Australian. Life is good in the Land of Oz, and I am lucky to call this place home. Australia is now "to the contrary belief of many," one of the most open economies in the world, and the country welcomes foreign direct investment (FDI). Hundreds of billions of dollars have been invested into the Australian economy over the last decade. Politicians from both sides of politics have made significant progress in opening Australia's doors to international businesses with what I believe to be a fairly attractive corporate tax rate with great benefits to business owners and foreign investors.

I believe that Australians generally have limitless opportunities. There aren't too many countries in the world where an individual can work at a fast food chain and make more than $7 per hour. Employees make more than double that at an Australian McDonalds. Australia is still a country where you can prosper with very limited education. Just think how many mine workers across Australia are paid more than $700 a day—without having a high school diploma.

Over the last several years, money has simply poured into the Australian economy on the back of a once-in-a-lifetime natural resources boom. Australian individuals have been spending that money like there is no tomorrow within the domestic economy. Australia has more iron ore than it will ever be able to export and a wealth of agricultural goods that is sold worldwide at a premium. Cities like Sydney and Melbourne have become increasingly recognized as regional and global business hubs. The states of Queensland and Western Australia have been the prime beneficiaries of the natural resources boom, and individuals from all over the country and the world have headed to some of the hottest deserts on earth to grab their small but valuable piece of the pie.

Although creeping higher, unemployment is still very low, and household wealth has increased significantly. The family home has never been more valuable, and is increasing in value, due to an apparent housing shortage. Australian property prices are among the highest in the world. Property investors, developers and real estate agents are profiting significantly. In Australia, its acceptable to run your property investment at a loss because the capital gain will be greater than the amount of money you pour into the property.

The Australian financial services industry is the most profitable in the world. Known as the "Big 4," The Commonwealth Bank, National Australian Bank, ANZ and Westpac are the largest financial institutions in Australia. As of February 2013, by market capitalization, the Big 4 make up four of the twenty largest banks in the world. They are the primary drivers of the domestic economy, offering loans to the private sector at all scales of the economy. The majority of loans in Australia go to the housing and mining sectors. Governments of recent time have commended the banks on their responsible lending practices.

At face value, the Australian economy is dynamic. Its largest trading partner, China, is an economic powerhouse that just keeps growing. Chinese government economists are incredible. Without fail, they predict how much their economy will grow each year with very little error. Australia has been, and will be, incredibly dependent on the Chinese growth story. China will be Australia's largest customer of natural resources and other raw products, including agriculture, for decades to come.

The Reserve Bank of Australia (RBA) has successfully managed Australia's interest rates to protect the economy from high inflation during an unprecedented near quarter of a century of economic growth. Yes—Australia has not had a recession since the early 1990s.

In a nutshell, while the majority of western nations— including the United States and the bulk of Western Europe—have endured several years of economic pain, Australians have been laughing while powering through tons of the finest seafood and building family wealth like never before. London and New York historically have become relatively cheap holiday destinations for Australian travelers. Australians have discovered high-end fashion and have become coffee and wine connoisseurs. Top-of-the-line models of BMW, Mercedes-Benz, and even Rolls Royce have become more visible on the streets of Australian cities.

Any Australian under the age of twenty-three has never seen an Australian recession. Any Australian born after 1984 probably can't remember that in 1990 the then-Treasurer of Australia, Paul Keating (who would one day become prime minister) called the 1990-91 recession "the recession we had to have." Prior to and during the recession, the then-Prime Minister, Bob Hawke, laid a foundation with Paul Keating for a new Australian economy. More importantly, Australian businesses, individuals and banks who got burned by lending rates as high as 17%, would forever be more cautious. It was around this time that the Hawke government began to make the great shift from economic protectionism to a more free-functioning economy. This included privatizing the financial services industry. In 1996, a John Howard-led Liberal Party came to power, defeating Paul Keating's Labor Party in a landslide victory election. With Treasurer Peter Costello at Howard's side, they worked aggressively and proactively to manage the Australian economy. The taxation system was modified, and Australia's public sector debt was being paid off and reduced to a very minimal level relative to GDP (sub 10% of GDP). In my opinion, prior to and post the early 1990s recession, Australia had great leaders and economic managers from both sides of politics until 2007.

Apart from Chinese nationals, there are not many individuals today who can say they've never lived through a recession. One third of Australia's population can. There are few employees in this world earning a minimum full-time salary of $622 per week. Every full-time employed Australian who is on minimum wage can proudly say that. Australia's minimum salary is equivalent to the GDP per capita of the European Union.

The dynamic Australian economy has also proved its resilience through some of the toughest global economic conditions. The economy grew during the Asian financial crisis, the dotcom bubble, and the global financial crisis. The Australian economy, for one reason or another, manages to dodge the recession bullet—a lucky country indeed.

Looking Beyond Face Value

What I have said thus far makes Australia sound like an incredible place to invest, do business and prosper. For the last twenty years, that has definitely been the case. A lot has changed since the last recession, including the ideology that is drilled into the mindset of the majority of the Australian population. However, when you peel back the face value of the Australian economy, you see a much different picture.

Through the course of this book, I will illustrate how the good times are going to come to an abrupt end. In my eyes, the evidence is becoming ever more compelling that the Australian economy is on track to go bust—and go bust in the very near future.

The Australian economy has made an enormous bet on what I like to call **The Three Pillars of the Australian economy**. Financial Institutions, Natural Resources and Real Estate are the three industries the Australian economy cannot live without. This book will show how deeply intertwined and connected the three pillars of the Australian economy are, and how they can easily take each other down in a domino-like effect.

11

If I were a betting man, I would bet that at least one of the Big 4 banks will either go bust as Lehman Brothers did in 2008, or will be bailed out or nationalized by the Australian government at a huge cost to the Australian economy and confidence. Up to three of the five largest miners in this country will also go bust. And the Australian property market will crash, placing more Australians in bankruptcy than ever before. Scary thought, isn't it? I have yet to hear many financial analysts addressing this very real possibility, but this could be Australia's reality in the next twelve to thirty-six months.

Australia, and its domestic mindset, is completely unprepared for any shock to the Australian economy. Australian economists assume that China's command-driven economy will continue to grow its construction sector for years to come. But what's the prime ingredient for China to continue expanding construction? Australian-dug iron ore. Has anyone seriously asked what would happen if the Chinese economy came to a screaming halt? Have you been to a third- and fourth-tier city in China to see how many cranes cover the polluted skylines? Well, that is where I believe the embryo of Australia's economic collapse is developing.

Chapter Two

Apples and Oranges

I've just moved back to Sydney after spending nine years living in Europe. In 2004, I moved to the beautiful Swiss village Epalinges, located just on the hilly outskirts of Lausanne in the Vaud Canton. And in 2010, I moved to the plush Central London neighborhood called St John's Wood. Throughout my time in Europe I traveled frequently to the U.S. (primarily to Houston and New York) and China for work. I was also very fortunate during my time in Europe to visit Australia two to five times a year.

There is a good chance that you have never heard of Epalinges—and that's the way the residents of this beautiful part of the world like it. Nestled within a Swiss forest, Epalinges is five-square kilometers of extreme yet discrete European wealth—including "Mr. Ikea," Ingvar Kamprad—residing on and around a picturesque golf course. Surrounding these beautiful places of abode are modest Swiss-style homes, and paddocks for cows to roam in the summertime. The Swiss Canton of Vaud is also known as a haven for billionaires and multimillionaires. Why is such extreme wealth packed into such a small area? The answer is simple. Taxes. Some of the richest non-Swiss individuals living in the Canton of Vaud pay tax based on the value of their properties and the rental value of that property (called the forfeit tax). Ingvar Kamprad was paying roughly $90,000 in taxes a year living in Epalinges. However, the remaining 99% of the residents of Canton Vaud are paying ordinary taxes in the same way the average American- or Australian-based worker does. The cost of living in Vaud is very high. A Big Mac meal at McDonalds will run you about AUD$11. GDP per capita in Vaud is around USD$77,000. And Geneva is just a forty-minute drive down the freeway. Geneva's population density is thirty-two times that of Sydney.

Similarly, Central London has arguably the highest concentration of Ultra High Net Wealth (UHNW) individuals in the world. A UHNW Individual is classified to be a person with a net (not gross) wealth in excess of $30 million. In London there are more than 4,000 of them. The cost of real estate in Central London is exceedingly high. And the population density in the Greater London area is thirteen times that of Sydney. Why are there so many UHNWs living in London? Two reasons. First: taxes. Second: it's one of the top global hubs and capitals for business, finance and transport.

The U.K. has a special tax regime for foreigners who wish to reside within its jurisdiction. You have the right to reside in the U.K., but you can choose not to be domiciled in the U.K. A U.K. resident non-domicile (non-dom) is not obliged to pay U.K. tax on non-U.K. derived income unless an individual brings offshore income or capital gains into the jurisdiction. Furthermore, the U.K. has a deregulated property market. Anyone from anywhere can go to the U.K. and buy property. London is the prime beneficiary of the non-dom tax regime and the influx of foreign cash to purchase property within the Central London area. Believe me when I say there's an extraordinary amount of wealth in London. When living in St John's Wood, I really began to understand how much wealth there is in this world, although hardly any of this wealth looked like it was stored in the hands of the Brits. It was mostly Middle-Eastern, African and Russian wealth. London is generally the first city that comes to mind for a wealthy emerging market individual should financial or political instability hit home. For these individuals, purchasing London property is their insurance policy and a potential roof over their heads in what truly is a safe haven.

Across the Atlantic you have New York City. In my opinion, New York City is the capital of the world. People from all over the world dream of, and come to, this grand and beautiful city in pursuit of dreams. And if there is any city in the world where you can make your dreams come true, New York is the first city that will come to mind. Just like London, New York is a global hub for finance, business and pretty much everything else. There are more billionaires living in New York than in any other city in the world. In the borough of Manhattan alone there are more than seventy billionaires. New York has a population density twenty-eight times that of Sydney.

New York and London share a wealth of similarities. However, the one big difference is taxation on residents of foreign abode. Anyone who lives in the United States is subject to American tax law. This means that if you live in the United States, you are subject to be taxed on your worldwide income. But does this matter? In my opinion, not really. New York is the hub of the world's biggest economy, and it proved its resilience as an economy and, more importantly, as a city after September 11, 2001. The city also proved its resiliency through the global financial crisis.

Houston, Texas, is the energy capital of the world. This city is packed with talent; it has one of the world's largest pools of highly skilled engineers, researchers and medical practitioners. The greater metropolitan area of Houston is huge and spans as far as the eye can see. Unlike New York, London and Geneva, the city has fewer apartments and more houses. And the metropolitan area is growing fast. In the last ten years, the population of Houston grew by more than 1.2 million. To put into perspective how quickly this city is growing, New York, Los Angeles and Chicago combined grew by 1.3 million over the same ten-year period. The city of Houston has a population of 2.16 million, and a population density nine times that of Sydney. The metropolitan area of Greater Houston, which includes neighboring cities, has a population of 6.2 million and a population density roughly 70% of Sydney's population density.

My renewable energy company GreenRigCo has its tiny office in the Woodlands-Spring neighborhood of Houston. It is a beautiful part of the world. I call it The Shire of Houston because of its resemblance to the Sutherland Shire in Sydney. Thirty-five minutes north of downtown Houston, the Woodlands-Spring area has some of the best golf courses in the United States, and the neighborhood has a median household annual income of $105,000.

Of all the cities in the world that I know well, I would say Houston is the city where I believe the economic fundamentals and cost of living makes the most sense. Now lets look at Australia.

Sydney is a city that consistently ranks in the Worldwide Top 10 for quality of life—and I agree. Sydney has the most beautiful waterways of any big city, and the beaches are sparkling clean. There are not many international cities that can offer similar geography, with its downtown area a short fifteen-minute drive from the beaches.

Sydney is physically huge. It spans as far as the eye can see, and there is a neighborhood for everyone. Want to be hip and trendy? You have Surry Hills and Newtown. Want to live beach culture at its best? The northern and southern beaches of Sydney are outstanding. Want to keep up with the Jones's? You have the Eastern Suburbs. The city spans well west of these areas, with neighborhoods of incredible multicultural flare and great food and identity reaching all the way to the edge of the Blue Mountains.

Sydney is also the economic hub of Australia. It's Australia's financial center, having the most global investment banks physically present, and by population it is the largest city in the country. Sydney airport is one of the most convenient airports in the world for location.

Sydney is an incredible melting pot of influence from all around the world. And there is some wealth in this city. Its relatively close proximity to Asia and similar time zone make it an attractive Western city to engage the Asian continent. Many wealthy Asian entrepreneurs and politicians send their children to Sydney and other major cities in Australia to study and enjoy a safe, relaxing life.

Sydney is now also recognized as being one of the most expensive cities in the world to reside. It will cost you more to live in Sydney than it would to live in New York (50% more), London (25% more)—and it is only slightly cheaper than Geneva (8% less). Australian law generally prohibits foreigners who do not reside in Australia from purchasing existing dwellings. Foreigners, however, are allowed to purchase vacant land, newly built homes, and under special circumstances, an existing dwelling.

Let's compare

I don't generally compare apples and oranges, but if I were to guess which city Sydney shares the most similar characteristics with out of Geneva, London, New York and Houston, I would say Houston. In terms of cost of living, however, it is closest to Geneva. So why do Australian journalists love to compare Sydney with New York and London? Beats me. Let's be very frank here. When it comes to economic fundamentals, Sydney is definitely no London, New York or Tokyo. According to the Brookings Institution, the GDP of Tokyo is higher than Australia's entire GDP. You simply cannot find an equation that gives relative reasoning to make a fair comparison between these cities, apart from them all being the major economic hubs of their countries.

In 2013, several different sources, including CNBC, rated Sydney as one of the ten most expensive real estate markets in the world. But when you think of other cities on that list—including New York, London, and let's include Hong Kong—they all have similar characteristics. The cost per square meter of real estate is exceptionally high, but the daily cost of living is not what I believe to be unreasonable. However, the daily cost of living in Melbourne,

Brisbane, Adelaide and Perth is higher than it is in New York. Yes! It costs more to live in Adelaide than it does to live in New York. And now that I am living back in Australia, it almost seems like Aussies are proud of the high cost of living. Why?

In relation to the cost of living, Sydney and Melbourne share similar cost-of-living characteristics as Geneva, Tokyo and Zurich. Yet Australian cities—by area, geography, population and economic focus—are more similar to the greater metropolitan areas of Houston, Miami and Dubai. During the Global Financial Crisis (GFC), Miami, L.A. and Dubai were among the most notable of cities to feel the true brunt of a collapse in housing prices.

The GDPs of Houston ($399b) and Miami ($292b) are higher than the GDPs of Sydney ($203b), Melbourne ($172b) and Perth ($102b). Relative to breadth, the GDPs of Australian cities are fairly similar to those of Miami and Houston. But why are Australians paying so much more for their properties, food and other daily essentials?

Out of whack

The following chart shows the median house price and median household income of select metropolitan areas (based on research by Demographia).

City	Population	Median Household Income (USD)	Median House Price (USD)	House Price vs. Household Income Ratio
Miami	5,502,379	$47,500	$252,200	5,3
Houston	4,944,332	$57,000	$186,000	3,2
Adelaide	1,225,235	$58,092	$368,480	6,3
New York	19,831,858	$65,200	$405,400	6,2
London	8,173,194	$67,200	$489,000	7,3
Melbourne	4,246,345	$66,552	$559,770	8,4
Tokyo	35,682,460	$70,666	$311,555	4,4
Sydney	4,627,345	$75,670	$679,338	9

Before I proceed, it must be noted, in relation to the above chart, that the average dwelling sizes in cities like London and Tokyo are significantly smaller than those in American and Australian cities. But once again, Sydney is no Tokyo, London or New York. Yes, London, New York and Tokyo have very expensive properties in their city centers. But prices do decline very rapidly the further a dwelling is from a city's prime real-estate locations.

What is interesting about this table is that there is not much of a trend. When analyzing property-price-to-household-income ratio, the differences are very clear. Houston has the lowest property-price-to-income ratio—just 3.2 times (3.2x) the household income. In London, it's 7.2x the income. Sydney's price-to-income ratio is at 9x. Is this out of whack, or what?

Property taxes are what generally moderate Houston's property market. You can pay up to 3% property tax annually in some the city's neighborhoods. Likewise, to a lesser scale, Miami and New York. Australian cities have land taxes for investment properties, and high upfront stamp duty taxes based on the purchase price of a dwelling. And if you're a foreigner in London and you want to buy a dwelling for more than £2 million, expect to pay 15% stamp duty on your property. But London does have by far some of the lowest annual property/council taxes in the Western world. You can live in a £25 million house in central London and you will only pay £1,361 annually in council taxes. Live in a pad worth a hundred times less and your yearly council tax will be £225 less than that of your well-heeled neighbor. But for local Londoners, the stamp duty rates are comparable to Australian rates. And if you're the renter, you're responsible for paying the council tax. However, in essence, taxes do not really affect the overall price of property. The city where taxes affect the overall property price the most on the above list is Houston. Imagine if the median property price in Houston was 9x the annual income. The average household would be paying $10 to 15k a year in property taxes.

Regardless, it is clear that Australians are paying a much higher relative price for real estate. The median house price in Adelaide is almost as expensive as that of New York. I would love to see the mayor of Adelaide stand in front of the world press and explain why Adelaide property prices are fair and good value, and that Adelaide has more opportunity and access to market than does New York. I would guess the first line of defense would be that you can't compare apples and oranges. But to the rest of the world, property prices in Adelaide would simply seem way out of whack.

It's easier to recognize a property bubble when you're looking at it from the outside. Just ask a long-term resident of Miami, Los Angeles, Dubai, Tampa, Detroit, Dublin, Atlanta, Barcelona, Las Vegas, Phoenix, Tokyo . . . the list goes on. What would a long-term Los Angeles resident think if he went house hunting in Sydney? Not long ago, a good friend from L.A. popped into Sydney for a visit and we drove around the city and had a look at the few properties for sale. We were standing in front of a very modest 3-bedroom home, when he pulled out his phone calculator to try to make sense of the math. I'll never forget his absolute bewilderment. He shook his head and muttered, "Dude, this is a bubble like I've never seen before. I just bought a 3-bedroom home in Beverly Hills for the same price as this piece of sh*t." Foreigners are truly blown away when they come to Australia and see how much it costs to live in The Lucky Country. After nine years living abroad, I could not agree more with these foreign visitors.

Once again I am not one to compare apples and oranges. But when you've been living, working and visiting major global cities, you just can't help it. Out of all the cities that have shocked me the most in terms of cost of living or visiting, Australian cities easily take the cake. One only has to look at the 2013 Concur Expense IQ Report to dive deeper into the pit of flabbergasted bewilderment. Four of the ten most expensive cities to host a business trip (excluding airfare) are in Australia. Brisbane is the most expensive city in the world to go for a business trip—excluding airfare! Can you believe it? Brisbane? Tokyo was second, followed by Sydney, Perth, London, Stockholm, Melbourne, Zurich, Paris and Dubai. The average cost for a business trip in Brisbane is $547.53 per day. The daily cost for a business trip to London is $516.46 per day. I cannot help but shake my head in dazed confusion. It costs $75 more per day to go on a business trip to Brisbane than it does to go to New York. It costs

$200 a day more than it does to go to Chicago. This is insanity. And it would not surprise me if the residents of Brisbane had their moment of glory ranking first for something in the global spotlight. Believe me, Brisbanians, this is nothing to be proud of.

Australia—its citizens, politicians, treasury departments, journalists and real estate bodies—can try to justify the reasoning of Australia's high cost of living and real estate as much as they want. But at the end of the day, there must be a reason why a country with a population density of less than three people per square kilometer has become such an expensive place to live and visit. Once again you cannot compare apples and oranges, but Australia is not that different to anywhere else—is it?

What is it that makes Australian real estate so expensive? Supply vs. Demand? Housing Shortage? High wages?

None of the above.

Can the Australian economy come crashing down?

Absolutely.

Chapter Three

Ignorance, Familiarity and Misinformation

The Pundits

For years, I have been listening to Australia's "never going to have a recession" pundits—Australian citizens, politicians, treasury departments, journalists, Big 4 CEOs, real estate bodies and mining giants. They tell the good people of Australia and the world that things are different in Australia. Yes, "different." Here are a few standouts.

"There is a chronic housing shortage in Australia based on demand exceeding supply."

"The American banks were lending recklessly. Australian banks are responsible lenders."

"Australians have the largest homes in the Western world, so it's a very different asset class in Australia versus other jurisdictions."

"A lot of commentators particularly over here (the U.S.) don't understand the Australian housing market."

"China will continue to need more Australian iron ore." "Australia has the safest banks in the world with their AAA rating."

The above statements clearly describe how the majority of the Australian public, industry and government feel about how "safe" the Australian economy is. Pundits simply assume that Australia is immune from any type of economic impact. Australians have accepted the idea that the statements above are fair and accurate judgments about the risks that lie within the Australian economy. Essentially, these statements are in direct relation to the Three Pillars of the Australian economy: Financial Institutions, Mining and Real Estate. For years it quite frankly has not mattered how Australia's manufacturing or retail industries have performed. Apart from the period between August 2013 to March 2014, these two industries have declined over the last several years. This has not stopped the Australian economy from growing; the Australian government and global investors are not focused on these industries in relation to Australia's economy. Natural Resources, Financial Services and Real Estate are the three industries that grew the Australian economy to the heights it is today. In my opinion, these are also the industries that will take the Australian economy down to the new lows of the near future.

Misinformation

In my opinion, the pundits have truly misinformed the Australian public. Australia is a democratic and free society. The press is allowed to communicate its "view" to Australians. However, when it comes to real estate and mining, there is a clear lack of objectivity.

For research and a great laugh, I read the property section of the Sydney Morning Herald (SMH) on the

Internet. I'm not sure who pays the income of SMH's real estate journalists, but it sure seems like they are supporting rising housing prices. Not just because house prices are rising, but also because there is an interest for one reason or another that property prices keep rising.

"Sydney property boom drives prices up by $100,000."

"Record-breaking Sydney auction market to end [year] on a high."

"Auction fever spreads to top-end property."

"Busiest February for auctions on record as owners rush to sell."

"Records smashed on Sydney's famous laneway."

When I read these headlines and the attached articles, it almost feels like the journalists are cheering rising property prices. Journalist Stephen Nicholls takes the cake at SMH. Why? Because he runs an article between a Saturday evening and a Monday morning headlining the auction clearance rate of Sydney's property market from the weekend:

"Unrenovated one-bedder on 51 sq. m fetches $745,000 as clearance rate hits 84.4%."

This was written on Saturday, February 8, 2014—about an hour after data unveiling the preliminary auction results for the week were made available. **Preliminary results are not final results**. Each week, SMH and other newspapers headline the preliminary results of auctions in Sydney and elsewhere in Australia. But they very rarely mention in their articles that their data is only based on preliminary results. Additionally, you never see much commentary on why a particular house was not able to sell at a particular auction. Basically, each week, real estate agents inform one of the privately owned real estate bodies—such as Australian Property Monitors (APM)—whether the properties they were auctioning sold or not. Several days later, by the time APM has collected the entire sample—which is never 100% of all auctions, they always release a smaller auction clearance figure than the preliminary result. Without fail, the preliminary auction results are always higher than the official auction results. Why? Because real estate pundits in general probably want to show strong sales data. If you're a real estate agent and you hold an auction whereby the property was passed in (not sold) because there were no bidders or no bidders willing to pay the reserve price set by the property owner, would you want to rush off and advise APM that you were not able to sell the property? Not really. But if you're a real estate agent and you hold an auction and the property sells, would you rush to give APM the good news? Absolutely.

Here is a clear example of the spin of the preliminary auction results: Saturday, February 22, 2014, I attended two auctions held by McGrath Realty in the southern beaches of Sydney. The first auction was for the sale of a sad-looking, 2-bedroom house in much need of a bulldozer in the suburb of Caringbah. It sold under the hammer for $926,000. That's a lot of money for an old 2-bedroom house with a modest backyard. The second auction was for a house in Dolans Bay. It was a bigger house than the first auction, but the crowd was smaller and there was

27

only one bid for $950,000. The auctioneer did not accept that bid because the price was deemed too low. The auctioneer asked the bidder if he could bring his bid up to $1 million. The bidder declined, and then there was a vendor (owner of the house) bid of $1.25 million. Heads shook, and the property was passed in. Later that evening when APM released the preliminary auction results, the house that was sold in Caringbah by McGrath was added to the preliminary result. The house that McGrath did not sell in Dolans Bay was not included in the preliminary result. There are only three possible reasons why the house that did not get sold did not make it into the preliminary auction results. Either McGrath Realty advised the APM of the sale of one house and didn't mention the failed sale until a later date, or McGrath advised of the results from both auctions and APM left out the failed sale in the preliminary results, or, in the name of maintaining a high auction clearance rate, both parties deliberately wanted to leave the failed sale out of the preliminary auction results.

I can't say that all newspapers take the same approach (reporting preliminary results in a way that indicates them to be final sales), because there aren't enough hours in a day for me to read all Australian newspapers. But, for one reason or another, SMH's property section is rushing strong auction clearance-rates data to readers of their property section. By the time the full auction results are gathered, the previous week is forgotten news and won't make the news again until twelve months later, when they compare the full auction clearance rate twelve months prior to the most recent preliminary result.

Dr. Andrew Wilson is the chief economist at APM. He also writes articles in the property section of SMH. On a Thursday or Friday he will write an article mentioning how many auctions will be held over the weekend. Forty-eight hours later, APM (his employer) always releases the auction results with fewer results than actual auctions held. If APM can find out how many houses are going to be auctioned on a particular weekend, it should not be any harder to get the results of all the auctions. It hurts to see that the average reader puts his or her faith and trust in Wilson's commentary. At worse, his readers make the biggest financial decisions of their lives and purchase properties because Wilson is telling them that based on supply and demand, the market will go higher. The only credit I can give Dr. Wilson is that he doesn't completely talk up the market like Mr. Nicholls does. But 90% of the time he does. Generally, the only time SMH reports official results is when they compare the preliminary data from the most recent weekend and the official data (which is always weaker) from a year earlier. SMH and APM are both owned by the Fairfax Media Group, which, for one reason or another, seems to influence the ways in which they represent real estate to their audience.

Aquasia's credit strategist, Mark Bayley, raised public awareness of the misleading headlines that were being plastered across Australia's newspapers. He wrote an article on the Financial Review: "Lies, dammed lies and auction clearance rates." He was the first analyst to really make a public statement on the flawed data coming from APM and newspapers such as SMH. Since then, APM has made slight modifications to the preliminary data they release.

So what happens with this data that APM releases every Saturday evening? It gets spun like there's no tomorrow. Real estate agents remind buyers that auction clearance rates are through the roof and demand is high. Potential homebuyers rush to their calculators to see if they're able to borrow more from the bank. Banks jump for joy because the size of the mortgages they will have to give to homebuyers will be larger than those of the previous month and year. So you have two of the three pillars (real estate industry and financial institutions) telling the general public that there is no better time to buy property than now. Throw the lowest interest rates in modern history into the mix, and you have a so-called property bonanza. In 2013 alone, the average property price apparently rose by $100,000 in Sydney. Any mention of a bubble gets quickly squashed by these two pillars that have enormous vested interest in property prices only going up and up. The same goes for their powerful network who work at the major newspapers that have the same vested interests.

In September of 2013, although shocked, I was not surprised when I read SMH's article on the average home-loan size in the state of New South Wales (NSW) that headlined, "Boom time as average home loan crosses $500,000." It goes on to say:

> "The executive general manager retail at National Australia Bank, Vicki Carter, said there had been a renewed interest in real estate, particularly among investors following the Reserve Bank's decision to cut rates to record lows last month."

Renewed interest? Judging by the articles in Australia's newspapers over the last few years, there was never any loss of interest. And look at the size of that average home loan in the state of NSW! More than $500,000! In my opinion, that is just an insane amount of money for an average home loan in any property market in any place in the world.

Ignorance

When you read that the average home loan in NSW is now more than $500,000 and interest rates are their lowest in modern history, you must wonder what the Reserve Bank of Australia (RBA) chairman, Glenn Stevens, must be thinking. The first thought that pops into my mind, and the minds of most foreign visitors, is the word, "Bubble."

Australian real estate journalists, and those with vested interest in real estate, love to use the word "Boom." But never will you hear the word that is always associated with every boom: "Bust." Glenn Stevens has been the chairman of the RBA since 2006. He was the chairman in 2008 when the global financial system crashed—when Australia was thrown the most valuable lifeline in its economic history. China pumped USD$800 billion into its own economy, and it has spent the last several years building more housing and infrastructure than it as a country may ever need. The grand beneficiary of this was Australia's second pillar: the natural resources industry.

This lifeline could not have come at a more desperate hour for Australia's economy. In 2008, the

Australian economy was starting to tumble to a point where some of the largest companies in the mining industry were ready to telephone the eagerly awaiting insolvency administrators and lawyers. With the Chinese government announcing historic measures to stimulate the Chinese economy through essentially investing in construction activities, Australia was spared from two consecutive quarters of negative growth and recession. From that moment, it was full steam ahead for the Australian economy—as if nothing at all was happening while Europe and America were deleveraging.

I believe the moment that China made the grand capital (printed money) injection into its economy was the moment that the Australian economists became ignorant; they lost touch with reality and began to use useless metrics and data to calculate and justify that the private-sector debt load would forever be manageable. All $1.9 trillion of it. Australia's political leaders and reserve bankers got cocky and fell asleep at the wheel. The only reason Australia lived through the GFC recession-free was by a stroke of luck. Australia had more iron ore than it will ever know what to do with. The weeks before the Chinese government pumped steroids into its economy, the Australian mining sector was on the verge of collapse. You just have to go back to the stock price chart of any major Australian mining company to see how bad it was getting in 2008. If the second pillar, the Natural Resources Industry, had collapsed in Australia back in 2008, it would have caused a house of cards moment, just as it did in the United States, the United Kingdom, Spain and Ireland. Why? If the mining companies (Pillar Two) collapse, the Australian dollar goes into absolute free-fall because there's nothing to export. If there's nothing to export, there's more money going out of the country than coming in. This means that the cost of foreign-made goods rises sharply (inflation). The RBA didn't want to raise interest rates any higher than they were at the time (7.25%) because that would send too many homeowners and businesses with big debts into bankruptcy. If too many individuals and business go bankrupt, the Australian financial services industry (Pillar One) cannot pay its debt obligations to the capital markets where the majority of the debt was originally acquired. This causes a credit crunch as there is simply not enough available debt in the market, and the banks stop lending. If the banks stop lending to those wishing to purchase real estate (Pillar Three) in a market where the cost of property is on average 5x to 9x the national household income, the property market will collapse. The property market collapses because the enormous difference between property prices versus annual household income means that buyers need an incredible sum of debt to cover the massive difference between the deposit and the purchasing price of the property. Australian citizens, the financial services, and real estate industries (Pillars One and Three) have absolutely no clue of the scale of disaster that would have followed a collapse of the second pillar in 2008.

Mr. Swan had stated on multiple occasions that the strong fundamentals of the Australian economy were the reason Australia only had a single quarter of negative growth during the GFC. Rubbish. Australia was thrown a lifeline by China. Mr. Stevens put the pedal to the metal by reducing interest rates all the way down from 7.25% in 2008 to just 3% in 2009. What happened next was insane. Australians went back to their property shopping spree with the full support of the Australian financial services industry. Ultimately, Australia learned absolutely nothing from what happened in 2008 throughout the rest of the world.

The Australian economy definitely dodged a bullet—but at the critical cost of a society believing it was bulletproof. The value of risk is in the eye of the beholder. And in Australia, what is considered to be low risk is considered very high risk in most other Western economies. Not many American or German households annually earning between $80k to $100k today would feel comfortable taking out a $700k loan to buy a house—in their eyes it would seem too risky. Too much debt. In Sydney or Melbourne, a $700k loan for a household annually earning from $80k to $100k would be deemed a calculated investment. With this shifted context, a high-risk property investment starts to lose the feeling of being high risk. Unfortunately, when society and an economy come to believe themselves to be bulletproof, it generally means that the national mindset enters a dangerous belief of invincibility. And the standards that politicians and government-paid economists need to uphold when the bar needs to be raised higher year after year will generally lead to an ultimate economic catastrophe. The result? The increased risk that is added to household balance sheets and banks inevitably leads to the collapse of the three pillars of the Australian economy. And it would not surprise me if this happens sometime in the next thirty-six months.

In 2008, the Australian economy dodged a GFC bullet, but it was the opportunity of a lifetime for the Australian government to pop an over-inflated property and credit bubble. Why? Because Australia was practically 100% guaranteed that from 2008 to 2012 the Chinese economy would inhale all the natural resources Australia could possibly extract from the ground. And China did exactly that. The second pillar mining companies' profitability would have softened the pain of a housing crash by essentially buffering the first and third pillars from collapsing but supporting them during a deleverage event. Fewer jobs would have been lost over the long term, and government revenue would have increased due to there being fewer property investors negatively gearing their properties. Property prices would have declined significantly, and financial institutions would have felt some pain, but it would have reduced the over-leveraged private sector debt burden in Australia to a more reasonable level.

There is simply too much private sector debt in Australia. I have never heard an economist discuss the true calamity of Australia's private sector debt level. The average Australian household has more debt on its books than does the average household of any other country. Why on earth are Australian economists saying the Americans were lending recklessly? 2008 was Australia's golden opportunity to lean up its private-sector balance sheet. In my opinion, this was the first and only opportunity Australia and its political leaders had to safely manage and navigate a controlled market correction post 1991 recession.

I completely understand if a reader would accuse me of being ignorant. To say that it would have been better for Australia to dive into recession in 2008, one must acknowledge the serious consequences of such an act. Yes, there would have been a lot of suffering. A lot! But when I look at the sheer mass of private-sector debt in Australia today, any shock to the market now will have far greater consequences than such a shock would have had back in 2008. Australian households now have more debt than ever before. The more debt an individual has, the less room there is to wiggle out of a sticky situation if times get tough—and the second pillar cannot be thrown a second lifeline by the Chinese economy. China simply cannot build its way out of an already overdeveloped and overleveraged housing and infrastructure sector.

Chapter Four

The First Pillar: Financial Institutions

"Our banks are strong"... at least that's what we have been told.

Commonwealth Bank (CBA), National Australia Bank (NAB), ANZ and Westpac (WBC) are known as the Big 4 banks in Australia, controlling more than 80% of the domestic banking business. The Big 4 are incredible. Year after year, the Big 4 consistently generate higher profits without fail. The Big 4 are also delivering large dividends to their shareholders. More importantly, the Big 4 are primarily domestic-focused banks in a country of just 23.4 million people, and they are all ranked in the top 20 banks in the world by market capitalization. The Big 4 are incredibly profitable banks that have what one can consider to be reasonably equal market shares of the entire Australian banking industry. If you are Australian, there is a pretty good chance you have a bank account at one of the Big 4 banks. If you don't reside in Australia, there is a fair chance you have never heard of these banks before.

Of any industry in Australia, the banking system has been the most successful at extracting the most value from its clients. Go to a teller at the CBA and see what they extract from you when you exchange USD$2000. When I did, the CBA must have made at least $90 from the transaction. Do you want to take $100 from your NAB account using an ANZ ATM machine? You'll pay $2 to get access to your funds.

Certainly this is excessive, but it is also globally accepted. However, more importantly, the Big 4 make the majority of their profits from lending—particularly, home mortgages. The banks have "bet the bank" on Australian real estate and natural resources.

Based on my research, I believe that Pillar One is the most important pillar of the Australian economy, and that it got the Australian economy to where it is today. Why? Without the banks lending generously over the last several years, there was absolutely no possible way that Australian real estate could have become so expensive. Furthermore, the banking industry as a whole has made a big bet that real estate and mining industries will grow. More specifically, the banks have bet that the land and building value of existing real estate dwellings will "increase." And just as important, they've bet that the volume of iron ore and other natural resources sent to China will grow without there being a significant drop in iron ore prices from what is now (long-term) historic high levels.

The Big 4 are highly exposed to the other two pillars. Such significant leverage pumped into Pillars Two and Three generally increases the valuation of an asset related to those particular industries. Why? Because when a domestic financial system increases the amount of funds (debt for buyers) specifically available for customers to purchase assets for that particular industry, demand is stimulated or generated. This demand will generally outpace supply if there are more interested parties willing to purchase a particular asset. Using Pillar Three (real estate) as a hypothetical example, see the table.

House for Sale	Asking Price	Potential Buyers	50% Deposit	25% Deposit	20% Deposit	15% Deposit	10% Deposit
	$600,000		1	1	3	3	2
Min Deposit	10%	10	1	1	3	3	2
	15%	8	1	1	3	3	
	20%	5	1	1	3		
	25%	2	1	1			
	50%	1	1				

Imagine a 2-bedroom house for sale in the suburbs of Melbourne. The asking price is $600,000, and there are ten buyers interested in purchasing this particular house. Hypothetically, all interested parties have somewhere between $60,000 to $300,000 in cash saved to purchase a home. Now, if the various financial institutions are willing to lend to a homebuyer who has a deposit of 10% deposit or greater, the hypothetical property will have eight buyers who will be able buy the house. If you have only 10% of the home value as a deposit, you won't be able to buy the property because you won't be allowed to borrow extra for purchasing fees such as stamp duty. Hypothetically, with eight potential buyers, there is the ability to create greater demand for the particular property. Ultimately, the owner of this house would almost be assured that his property will be sold at the asking price—or, more often than not, at a price that is greater than the asking price.

Fast-forward twelve months: the hypothetical house in suburban Melbourne is for sale again. If the financial institutions in Australia (regardless of the reason) are "hypothetically" only now offering loans to those with a deposit of 30% or greater, there is only one prospective buyer with the ability to pay the asking price. If there is only one person with the ability to purchase the property, there is a good chance that this buyer will not be under pressure to act quickly, and he or she may be much less inclined to pay the asking price. There is a good chance the seller will be forced to reduce the selling price of the property, because there is probably more or equal supply in the marketplace than there is demand due to the fact that twelve months earlier there were eight buyers with the capacity to purchase the house, but now there is only one.

This leads to my point—and it's probably the most important point in this whole book. **In Australia, real estate prices do not depend on supply and demand; they depend on the banks willingness to lend excessively to homebuyers.** The more leverage the banks are willing to offer equates to higher demand. The less leverage the banks are willing to give equates to lower demand.

With the average loan in the state of NSW now exceeding $500,000 and the median home price being slightly higher than that amount, you don't have to be a financial analyst to see that the banks are taking on increasingly highly leveraged home loans relative to household incomes. In America, this was called "toxic lending."

A bank's balance sheet never lies

The following table contains some financial data from the balance sheets of six different banks. A balance sheet is a snapshot of the financial health of a bank at a particular point in time. It's important to be able to assess whether a bank is highly leveraged or not. Guess which banks they are?

	Total Cash (In Billions)	Total Long-Term Debt (In Billions)	Total Assets (In Billions)	Cash vs. Assets Ratio	Cash as % of assets	Cash-Debt Ratio	Cash as % of Long-Term Debt
Bank 1:	12,608	117,99	753,876	59.8x	1.67%	9.36x	10.69%
Bank 2:	38,306	122,744	808,427	21.1x	4.74%	3.20x	31.21%
Bank 3:	9,862	104,88	696,603	70.6x	1.42%	10.63x	9.40%
Bank 4:	39,129	91,57	702,991	18.0x	5.57%	2.34x	42.73%
Bank 5:	26,041	54,54	144,673	5.6x	18.0%	2.09x	47.75%
Bank 6:	20,029	123,15	691,063	34.5x	2.90%	6.15x	16.26%

First, look at Bank 1. It has $12.6 billion in cash. This cash is not the cash of depositors; it is the bank's cash. When Bank 1 pays a bill for stationary, it uses this cash. In a nutshell, if Bank 1 donated $12.608 billion to charity tomorrow and could not sell any of its securities to cover any of the shortfalls of the donation, it would be broke because it would have no cash to operate.

Now look at the "Total Long-Term Debt" column. That is the amount of long-term debt the bank has. Think of it like a 25-year home loan. For example, Bank 1 has $117.99 billion of long-term debt. If Bank 1 doesn't pay back that debt or its interest to its creditors, it will default its debt obligations and the creditors will come in—and the rest is history. It is done in just the same way that a bank will take away a house from a client if he or she cannot pay the interest and repayments for his or her home loan. Total Assets of the bank is the value of the assets that are generating the bank's income—for example, home loans. If a bank has given a client a $500,000 home loan, the $500,000 lent is classed as an asset on the bank's balance sheet. Why? The $500,000 loan is generating interest and profit for the bank. Bank 1 has 59.8x ($753 Billion) versus the available ($12.6 billion) cash on hand tied up in investments such as home loans. For whatever reason, if there is $12.6 billion in failed investments out of the **$753 billion**, the bank will probably run out of cash needed to run its business if it struggles to sell assets and pay back its creditors. In my view, this is a very high-risk profile bank.

Of the six banks on the list, I would say Bank 5 is the safest place for your deposits. Why? Because it has a low-risk lending profile. For every dollar of cash it has as a bank, it has only lent or invested 5.6x the available cash. Bank 5 also has only around twice the level of long-term debt versus its cash available to cover any losses.

If a savage financial storm equally affected these six banks, which ones would be the first to go bust? It would probably happen in this order: Bank 3, Bank 1, Bank 6, Bank 4, Bank 2 and Bank 5. Bank 5 is the safest because it has the least exposure to loans and investments that it has made versus its available cash. Bank 3 is the most exposed because it has, as a percentage, the least cash available relative to the amount of loans and investments it has made. If there was a severe financial shock and all banks were equally affected, Bank 3 would probably be the first to go belly up.

Ratios are great way to assess both the sustainability of a bank's business model and the level of risk a bank has taken in order to generate income and profits. In 2008, the world learned a valuable lesson from overleveraging. The more debt (assets) a bank issues to its customers, the less room it has to navigate through an economic downturn. The six banks in the table all have different Cash vs. Total Assets ratios. The higher the number, the more risk taken by the bank. Bank 1 has $12.6 billion in cash, but it has 59.8x that number locked up in investments, including home loans—and that is according to best calculation of the actual value of the asset in which the bank has invested. If Bank 1 makes a poor investment decision, or a shock hits the marketplace, the value of the bank's assets will decline, but the level of interest obligations and monetary value will remain the same for its customers as it does for the bank in regards to those who give it money to lend. They are the bank account holders, lenders to the bank and bond issuances. In a nutshell, if Bank 1 lends a $600,000 home loan to a person who wants to purchase a $700,000 house and 12 months later the house is worth $500,000, the lender cannot reduce its debt obligations, and neither can the bank to its own creditors. This is called a mortgage that is "underwater." An underwater mortgage is where the debt owed to a bank or creditor is greater than the value of the asset that the debt was used to purchase.

How do the Australian banks generate such large profits?

Who are Banks 1, 2, 3, 4, 5 and 6? The average Australians will be shocked with what they are about to read, because the majority of the Australian population has been misinformed about the real financial health of the Australian banking system. The reason banks in Australia are so profitable is because they have adopted what I like to call the LEHMAN MODEL! In other words, the Big 4 banks in Australia are incredibly profitable because they are highly leveraged financial institutions. In good times, when a bank is highly leveraged it will generally be highly profitable. However, the more leverage a bank has, the less room it has to navigate through risk when times get tough. Although the Big 4 banks in Australia are primarily retail banks, the level of risk taken by the Big 4 share similar characteristics to the financial health of the American financial services industry just prior to the GFC.

The table below unveils the identities of those six banks.

	Total Cash (Billions)	Total Long-Term Debt (Billions)	Total Assets (Billions)	Cash vs. Assets Ratio	Cash as % of assets	Cash-Debt Ratio	Cash as % of Long-Term Debt
Bank 1: **CBA** (2013)	12,608	117,99	753,876	59.8x	1.67%	9.36x	10.69%
Bank 2: **NAB** (2013)	38,306	122,744	808,427	21.1x	4.74%	3.20x	31.21%
Bank 3: **WBC** (2013)	9,862	104,88	696,603	70.6x	1.42%	10.63x	9.40%
Bank 4: **ANZ** (2013)	39,129	91,57	702,991	18.0x	5.57%	2.34x	42.73%
Bank 5: **Zurich Cantonal Bank** (2013)	26,041	54,54	144,673	5,6x	18,0%	2,09x	47.75%
Bank 6: **Lehman Brothers** (2007)	20,029	123,15	691,063	34,5x	2,90%	6,15x	16.26%

Does this look frightening? If you look at this table, you will notice that in 2013, all of the Big 4 had cash-to-asset ratios reasonably similar to those of Lehman Brothers fifteen months prior to its collapse in September of 2008 **(THE LARGEST BANKRUPTCY IN HUMAN HISTORY!).**

Australian banks are apparently regarded as "safe" financial institutions. Australian Big 4 CEOs, political leaders, real estate pundits, and account holders will tell you this and defend their views aggressively. But the numbers speak for themselves. And unless the banks are hiding something from their balance sheets (which is illegal) **the numbers do not lie**. Just because the credit agencies give Australian banks high credit ratings doesn't mean those banks are safe. Lehman Brothers and the credit instruments Lehman Brothers sold and supplied to the marketplace were regarded as safe in 2007. Essentially, WBC and CBA have risked a greater sum of cash—made available through deposits and interbank lending versus the cash the bank has on hand—than Lehman Brothers risked in 2007. CBA and WBC have effectively less cash than Lehman Brothers did fifteen months prior to its collapse, but CBA and WBC have lent (primarily for home loans) more money than Lehman loaned. Because the Big 4 have been able to grow assets on their balance sheets with uninterrupted year-after-year growth, the banks will become more profitable. However, if interrupted growth hits Pillars Two, Three, or both, they will quickly become highly exposed banks with little liquidity and little immediate collateral to protect their businesses from collapsing. They are simply overleveraged. To stay alive, CBA theoretically requires a 98.33% success rate and new immediate revenue in the investments it makes (including home loans). If this is not high risk, I don't know what is. There are not many businesses I am aware of that have a long-term 98.33% success rate on all the investments they make.

The profitable bank

CBA is Australia's largest bank by market capitalization ($120.7 billion). By the end of 2013, 77% of CBA's banking net income came from interest paid by its customers who had borrowed money. Mortgage customers of the CBA paid $16.8 billion in interest in just six months to December 2013 at a cost to CBA of $9.39 billion, or a 56% mark-up on lending from a slim margin business. Of the $709 billion in loans (interest-earning assets) that CBA has on its books, $387 billion (25% of Australian GDP) of that is tied up in home loans. You will find a similar story when you dive through the financials of the three other Big 4 banks.

When it comes to deposits and lending, banks are essentially the middlemen. In the simplest form, it is up to the Big 4 banks to decide what to do with the money you place in your bank account. Furthermore, banks have to buy the debt from other institutions and give their bank account holders and interbank lenders interest for the money they have in their accounts. It's not as though a bank lends and takes all the interest for itself as 100% profit.

In Australia, the money you place in a standard bank account (savings or deposit) will likely be consolidated with money from other bank deposit accounts and lent to prospective homebuyers. In return for depositing the money into the bank, the bank will offer you a piece of the pie in the form of interest. But your bank account balance will only show how much you have deposited and taken out of your own account, as well as the interest you have earned from letting the bank do what it wants with your money. And, yes, if you want to withdraw all the funds from your bank account, the bank will politely return the money to you in cash, or transfer the funds to another bank. At this particular point in time, Australian banks can afford to do this.

Loans to the private sector

Here is a hypothetical question. Imagine in the early stage of an economic downturn that there are two neighboring countries that have exactly the same economic dynamics, income per capita, population, characteristics and currency. Both economies have a GDP of precisely $1 trillion with 0% growth, 0% inflation and 4% interest rates at retail level. For the three years prior to the economic downturn, Country A grew by an average of 4% per year and Country B grew by an average of 2% year. The private sector debt in Country A is $1.2 trillion (120% of GDP), and in Country B it is $550 billion (55% of GDP). If a sharp economic downturn smacked both countries in exactly the same way, which of the two countries would feel the pinch more intensely? Which of the two private-sector economies would struggle more to pay its debt obligations if interest rates increase? If 66% of each economy's private sector debt was exposed to housing, which property market should collapse first if interest rates increase significantly? Which country would have higher property prices? Would the banks be more exposed to an economic downturn in country A or B? Theoretically, the added level of private-sector debt in country A would be more exposed to economic pain; it is no secret that those most exposed to leverage need to extract more of their income to repay more of their debts to creditors.

In this hypothetical situation, the private sector of Country A has more debt per capita. If interest rates at retail level in both countries were 4%, the private sector in Country A would be paying $48 billion (4.8% of GDP) a year in interest repayments, and

Country B's private sector would be paying $22 billion (2.2% of GDP). If the banks in Country A had been more willing than the banks in Country B to offer more leverage to the private sector, there is a good chance the asset valuations of real estate and businesses would be significantly higher in Country A than in Country B. If the currency of Country A and B depreciates, creating inflation, and there is a 1% rise in interest rates in both countries A and B (both with the same interest rate), Country A's private sector would now have to repay creditors an extra $12 billion a year in interest (1.2% of GDP). This would reduce the ability of Country A's private sector to grow and comfortably circulate cash throughout the country's economy. For Country B it would be $5.5 billion (0.55% of GDP) that would be extracted from the economy and paid to creditors. With less exposure, Country B, although negatively affected, would have $32 billion extra cash than Country A flowing through its economy.

In this hypothetical situation, what happens to the banks of Country A and B? What is clear is that the banks in Country A are in a lot more trouble than those in Country B. Why? Because banks in Country A have twice the exposure to private sector leverage during a period of financial hardship. If the private sector of Country A is now paying $60 billion a year in interest in a 0%-growth environment versus Country B's $27.5 billion, Country A's bank deposits start to become smaller. The bank deposits in Country A shrink faster than those in Country B because the private sector needs to pay a greater percentage of its GDP to interest repayments. With 0% growth, Country A's private-sector economy will lose confidence and start to shrink by about 6% per year versus country B's 2.7%. Both economies would most probably fall into recession. But Country A would suffer significantly more hardship than Country B would.

In this hypothetical situation, the banks in Country A start to find themselves in a dangerous situation. With bank deposits in Country A shrinking at a significantly faster rate than those in Country B, deposit holders become nervous about keeping their money in a Country A bank. Why? Because the banks in Country A are still exposed to $1.2 trillion of private sector debt, and there is an extremely strong chance that a proportion of private sector mortgage holders are either struggling to repay their debts or are already in the process of default. Unemployment also rises faster in Country A. The amount of cash the banks need to cover losses from defaults increases to a point where it is clear that the banks in Country A will soon run out of the cash necessary to cover their losses. If it becomes clear that this scenario is going to take place, depositors rush to withdraw their deposits. Essentially, you have **a run on the banks**. Depositors in Country A want to withdraw their funds in the Country A banks and deposit their funds in Country B's banks. Why? Although there is financial hardship in Country B, there is a much better chance that the banks in Country B will survive through this economic downturn because they have less exposure to defaults and financial hardship as compared to Country A's financial institutions.

If there is a run on the banks in Country A, the banks probably won't be able to repay their long-term debt obligations to their creditors, and they won't have enough money to cover the valuations of the loans they have lent to the private sector.

Essentially, the banks will run out of money and go bust. No economy wants to ever get to this point, as it is catastrophic to any economy—ask anyone who was living in Iceland between 2007 and 2010.

Pundits claim that the amount of private sector debt in Australia is manageable—all $1.89 trillion of it. The amount of $1.89 trillion is close to 20% more than Australia's **total** GDP.

The Australian private sector has taken an incredible amount of risk relative to the size of the Australian economy. The Big 4 banks are the creditors that own the bulk of the loans made to the private sector. Of all the loans to the private sector, the Big 4 and other Australian mortgage-lending companies have lent $1.4 trillion to households. Of all household debt, 90% is money borrowed by customers to purchase real estate. The remaining 10% of household debt is either personal debt or credit card debt. Banks in Australia have been exceedingly generous to households, lending an exorbitant amount of money. If all the household debt in Australia were equally divided by all Australian households (occupied and unoccupied), there would be $161,539 of debt per household. To put this into perspective, average household incomes in the U.S. and Australia are fairly similar, but Australian households have more than twice the amount of debt. Of course, every household in Australia does not have equal debt exposure. In general, the more recent a loan is taken to purchase real estate, the higher the level of debt exposure relative to income and equity value of the purchased property. And with housing prices in Australia deemed high versus relative incomes, the banks in Australia are highly exposed to one particular industry.

If the Australian economy either stagnates or enters a recession, the Australian economy is highly exposed to existing private sector leverage. Roughly 80% of this exposure is tied up in the Big 4 banks.

If Australia becomes exposed to a similar scenario that the hypothetical Countries A and B experienced, can the Australian banks weather the storm? Probably not—and for a lot of reasons that don't seem to be openly discussed in Australia. First, relative to scale, as in the hypothetical scenario, Australia has a similar exposure of loans to the private sector as does hypothetical Country A. Look what happened to the American, Spanish or Irish economy in 2008 when the realization set in. These economies tanked. The global financial system went into meltdown. Bear Stearns was acquired for cents on the dollar, and Lehman Brothers went bankrupt. Millions of Americans, Irish and Spaniards lost their homes. In the U.S., had it not been for the American government bailing out the banks that remained, most of the other major banks would have suffered the fate that Lehman did. This would have left America in an inconceivable position. And it would have taken the world with it. Remember, it wasn't public debt in America that caused the global financial crisis; it was loans made to the private sector. More specifically, it was loans made to homeowners.

The U.S. Financial Services Industry Was
Too Big To Fail.
In Australia, It's Too Big To Save

What leads me to believe there will be either the collapse, nationalization or bail out of "at least" one of the Australian Big 4 within the next thirty-six

51

months is the sheer potential calamity of the current situation. I also believe a handful of smaller mortgage lenders will also suffer the same fate. The Big 4 banks are among the most leveraged mortgage lenders in the Western world. Today, the Australian banking system has little cash on hand relative to the amount of assets and long-term debt that must be managed. For whatever reason, if Australia finds itself in a position where 0% growth or less is a reality, the country and its residents will finally be smacked with the truth of the size of Australia's overall private sector debt. Why? Because you rarely hear about the true seismic scale of loans made to the Australian private sector. Almost 100% of the time, Australians are told that Australian banks are safe—that they are well capitalized, and responsible lenders. Any contrarian views are quickly squashed by the powerful pundits. And in Australia, the powerful banking pundits have the trust and faith of the majority of the Australian public. Why? Because Australia has not had a recession in almost a quarter of a century, the view of risk has changed, and ignorance has set into the general mindset of the Australian public. Furthermore, and just as importantly, who has the bank been lending all this money to? The private sector. Does the private sector want to see the value of their assets become less than the leverage they have?

Once again, I don't like to compare apples and oranges; but the Big 4 banks are similarly, and more so, exposed to private sector debt as Lehman Brothers was fifteen months before it went bust on September 15, 2008. The big difference, which presents a whole other problem for Australia, is the sheer size of the Australian banks relative to the size of the Australian economy. In June 2007, Lehman

52

Brothers was holding more than $691 billion in assets. At that point in time Lehman's assets were equivalent to roughly 1/20th or 5% the size of the American GDP. The $691 billion bankruptcy sent catastrophic shockwaves throughout the American economy and the world. If CBA went bankrupt in Australia, it would be apocalyptic. Why? Because the assets in the hands of the CBA are equivalent to **48.5%** of Australia's GDP. Digest that for a second. America took a once-in-a-lifetime hit from a bank that went belly up with a 1:20 ratio of assets versus GDP. CBA has almost a 1:2 ratio.

Following Lehman's failure, the American Congress enacted the Emergency Economic Stabilization Act of 2008. The Emergency Economic Stabilization Act, also known as The Bailout, was established to purchase $700 billion worth of distressed assets held by the American financial services industry— equivalent to slightly more than 5% of America's GDP. If one of the Big 4 banks in Australia were to fail, could the Australian government make an equivalent bailout of up to 48% of GDP? Could the Australian government honor its pledge to guarantee Australian deposits up to $250,000 per deposit account? These are questions that have not been seriously assessed and answered.

If an economic shock hit Australia, sending the banks into financial mayhem, making property prices in Australia fall by 50%, and pushing the Big 4 banks to the verge of collapse, how would the Australian government find between $100 billion to $700 billion to buy distressed assets and to honor its commitment to guarantee bank deposits? Once again, its only when economic times get tough that Australians will realize the true scale of leverage that exists within the Australian private sector. And remember, the more leverage that a bank has pumped into the economy, the less room mortgage holders have to navigate through rough seas. At best, you end up hoping to ride out the storm.

If an economic storm hits Australia, the first pillar of the Australian economy will be severely punished for its risky lending practices. Remember—in a recession, those with the most debt at that particular point in time are at the most risk of default. **In the United States the financial services industry was too big to fail. In Australia, it's too big to save.**

Disneyland

When I read through all the comments made by the Australian banking pundits, I can't help but wonder if they're living in Disneyland. Why? Because today times are good; in fact, for the Australian financial services industry, times are "booming." The word "bust" is not even in their vocabulary. It's as if the GFC never happened.

In June 2013, SMH sported this headline: "CBA chief Ian Narev not losing sleeping over property bubble fears." Narev is quoted as saying, "I do not lose a moment's sleep thinking about that [property bubble]." Any friend of mine will tell you that I do what I can to avoid risk. In 2008, I was physically present in the major financial hubs in Europe and America to witness the biggest global financial crisis thus far in my lifetime. I was in New York on a business trip mid-September of 2008. You could see the bankers walking around with their hands on their heads and their eyes wide open in disbelief. Any meeting with a banker or financial institution that was not related to survival was cancelled. I saw Lehman employees walking out of their 7th Avenue office with boxes full of personal possessions and company stationery. In the months leading up to the Lehman collapse I would meet bankers indirectly emphasizing the true challenge at hand. After Bear Stearns was bought for cents on the dollar earlier in 2008, it was clear that hell was on its way. During this period I was a strategy and business development consultant primarily focused on helping clients improve growth models. On the behalf of my clients, I would liaise frequently with financial institutions to help bring new strategies to fruition. A few months before Lehman collapsed, I heard words that came out of the mouth of a leading banker from one of the largest investment banks in the world— words I will never forget:

> "Lindsay, debt [in the wholesale market] is becoming scarce and very expensive. It is unlikely that we will be able to provide our normal levels of financial service on behalf of the client."

When a very powerful banker tells you these words, you cannot help but feel confused and silenced. I left the meeting wondering why on earth a major financial institution would walk away from a dream low-risk, highly capitalized, "safe" business client that was a household name in their home country. If my client (with an extremely low debt profile) was unable to get access to the desired financial products and services in the capital markets, where did that leave the everyday Tom, Dick and Harry? My gut was telling me there was a serious problem in the global economy. I was watching airlines bleed money at the hands of record-high oil prices. Property prices and the Dow Jones had peaked in the U.S. and were now heading south.

It was at this point in time that I began to receive an unusual increase in enquiries from corporations requesting my assistance. Great! It was mind blowing! All phone enquiries started in almost exactly the same way: "Mr. David, we have a small problem, can you help us?" Never in my consulting career had I received so many phone calls regarding the same problem: **Access to credit**. Not so great! A lot of businesses and individuals were financially burned in an instant. And that was just the very beginning of it all. By August, I had witnessed a banker cry for the first, and certainly not the last, time. I was in New York when Lehman collapsed, and several days later I was in London. You could see the bankers were either tired or fired. You could see pain in their bloodshot eyes.

Fast-forward to 2014. After witnessing what I saw firsthand in 2008, I can say this with absolute clarity: If I was the CEO of a major bank that had hundreds of billions of highly exposed leverage, I would not sleep at night.

In February 2014, following another record-breaking profit result from CBA, Narev states:

> "The reasons we don't think we have a housing bubble is not just because a lot of the incidences of price rises are quite location specific, but also if you look at the fundamental dynamics of supply and demand,

the current levels of prices are well supported by levels of supply and demand."

What I believe Mr. Narev fails to mention at the end of this statement is that the banks' willingness to continue to give property purchasers increasingly higher loans relative to household incomes to pay for increasingly higher property valuations is what supports the high demand for real estate. Without the banks' willingness to lend more and more to real estate buyers, there is no possible or logical way that Australian house prices can maintain or gain in value. That is the root cause of the underlying strength of the third pillar of the Australian economy. But you will never hear a prominent Australian banker or mortgage lender such as Aussie Home Loans' CEO, John Symond, mention the root cause. They will just stick to the generic line that it's all about supply and demand. I strongly fear that CBA and WBC are not prepared for any shock to the Australian economy, just as Lehman or Bear Stearns was unprepared for any shock to the American economy.

As the first and most exposed pillar of the Australian economy, financial institutions are in what I believe to be a double-edged sword situation. If the second or third pillar of the Australian economy runs dry on demand, it will take the first pillar—the financial services industry—down with it. If the banks walk away from investing in the second or third pillar, the first Pillar will collapse.

What will bring the first pillar of the Australian economy into unchartered waters? There are a few possible triggers. The first possible trigger is that homebuyers will finally wake up to the fact that they are paying unreasonably high prices for dwellings. This is possible, but as long as the banks have access to credit and pass it onto the homebuyers, there will be enough growth in lending.

With such a high level of household debt—both as a percentage of household income and the sheer sum value—a 1% to 1.5% rise in interest rates could send the banks tumbling. But most likely, the embryo of the demise of the first pillar has already begun in hundreds of cities in a country 5,000 miles away.

Chapter Five

China

The Bubble to End All Bubbles

China is extraordinary. When I look back at my first trip to China in 1998 and compare it to how the country looks today, it is simply awe-inspiring. China has changed significantly in the last sixteen years. In 1998, China was raw. You could feel its culture and identity. There were some buildings over the skylines of Beijing, Shanghai and Guangzhou, but you could see en masse the traditional Chinese buildings and architecture. Fast-forward sixteen years—it's hard to explain how fast this country has grown since 1998. Back then, there were a handful of high-rise buildings, but nothing like the thousands of them that now cover the horizon. To put things into perspective, imagine downtown Adelaide. Imagine in just twenty years from now that the skyline will resemble that of Manhattan. In modern China, the traditional Chinese architecture is now barely visible in big cities, apart from a handful of important cultural buildings of importance. That's the best way to describe the change in China.

You might think that a quarter of a century is a long time without having a recession. Chinese statistics suggest that China has not had a recession since 1976. Earthquakes and drought caused that recession. Not only does the Chinese economy continue to grow year after year, it grows at an incredibly rapid rate. Since 1992, the Chinese economy has had yearly growth of somewhere from 6% to 14.2%. This is not just growth—it's hyper-growth. China has a command-driven economy. In relation to its economy, the Chinese government plays a very big role compared to the government's role in Western capitalist countries. The Chinese government owns most of the largest companies in the country. These companies are called State Owned Enterprises (SOE). From the 1990s to the middle of the last decade, manufacturing and exports were the prime economic drivers of the Chinese economy. Fast-forward to 2004—SOEs are now the backbone of the Chinese economy, and the prime industrial focus is investment in construction, infrastructure and real estate. This sector of the economy has taken over and become hands down the most important function of Chinese economic growth.

It must be noted that there is a lot of skepticism in relation to the financial data that is released by the Chinese government. Although I will leave this topic for others to argue over, it is generally more challenging to find extremely concrete data on China's economy. This is particularly relevant to trade and GDP. However, for this research, I will use official Chinese data and statistics and, as mentioned, leave the argument over the reliability of data for others to write about.

In the lead up to 2008's GFC, China's economy was growing by close to 13%. By 2009, China's growth had dropped down to around 6%. Any Western country would kill for 6% growth. As its economy was heading south as a result of the effects of the GFC, in November of 2008 China launched a USD$586 billion financial stimulus. Where did the bulk of that money go? Into investments related to the development of infrastructure and real estate. Who was one of the prime beneficiaries of this financial stimulus? The Australian mining industry. This financial stimulus was the mining industry's guarantee that the Chinese would need to purchase as much natural resources as it could get its hands on to build all of this new infrastructure and housing. If an industry as a whole was ever thrown a lifeline in the midst of calamity, this was it. Back in 2008, China was roughly a $4.5-trillion economy. In 2013, China's economy surpassed $9 trillion.

In just five short years, China's economy, in terms of size, has doubled. For an economy to grow this fast generally requires an incredible amount of investment as a proportion of GDP to be able to reach such high levels of growth. And that is what China has done. It invests relentlessly. I have tried time and time again to understand where all the money in China is coming from, and unless China is printing trillions, I have no clue. In 2012, there were only two countries in the world that spent more as a proportion of their GDP in fixed investments: The Republic of Congo (52% of GDP) and Sao Tome and Principe (49% of GDP). Fixed investments are 46% of China's GDP, i.e., if China's GDP was $8.22 trillion in 2012, roughly $3.7 trillion of that was fixed investments. Although China's economy grows fast, its internal rate of return is very poor. When you are investing 48% of GDP and only growing by 7 to 8% while increasing your investments year after year, you're doing something wrong. Once again, the bulk of these investments are made in infrastructure and property development. To spend trillions in constructing infrastructure and property development, you need steel. And you need a lot of coal to keep the highly polluting power stations in line with demand . . . unless all the new real estate developments and cities are empty.

When a country pumps trillions year after year into construction, you can imagine the number of cranes covering the skyline. Literally every city, and city that is in the process of being developed, has cranes everywhere. Drive the two hours from Guangzhou to Taishan, and you lose count in the first thirty minutes of the number of cranes that sit in the skyline between the two cities—and that's just on one road heading in one direction for 130 kilometers in a country of more than 1.3 billion people.

Today in China, you have a high-speed rail system, big modern airports and six of the ten busiest shipping ports in the world. New freeways are everywhere and, more importantly, there are residential apartment buildings as far as the eye can see.

If you are visiting China for the first time, you will be amazed at the visible level of construction that is taking place right across this big country. Several hundred cities you have never heard of are all aiming to become the most attractive locality for business investment and lifestyle. If you are ever in a third-, fourth- or fifth-tier Chinese city, go to one of their local investment bureaus and look at the master plan of that particular city. They all show you what's in store for that particular city. What a showcase it is! It's a new freeway! A new economic zone! A new stadium! There's a promotional video that makes that particular third- or fourth-tier city look like it's going to look like the city in the movie Total Recall. The city planners want to rival New York, Shanghai and Tokyo. You essentially have hundreds of cities all in incredibly aggressive competition for investment. When you walk out of a local investment bureau's showcase, you are either truly amazed or truly skeptical. If you believe in or know very little about the China growth story, you walk out of an investment bureau amazed. But if you've spent enough time traveling and doing business in various Chinese first- to fifth-tier cities, you have a pretty good understanding of the underlying challenges that China will one day face.

A lot of cranes in the skyline, but no people

Most of you by now have heard of the Chinese ghost towns. These are cities in China that are practically empty. Yes, empty in terms of population relative to the amount of residential dwellings. Have you ever seen the movie Vanilla Sky, where Tom Cruise is the only person in Times Square? It's something like that. Yes, there are a handful of people living in any city in China. But as a whole, the majority of China's third- to sixth-tier cities are looking emptier and emptier. To get the clearest picture of what I am trying to say, go to the CBS News website and watch the "60 Minutes" report on China's property bubble.

But just because a city in China might only be at 10% to 20% capacity, doesn't mean that no construction is taking place. To the contrary, construction is increasing. Why? Because the ultimate economic goal for China is growth. What makes the China growth story unique is that, like

Australia, China has created its own three pillars of economic growth: Construction, Construction, Construction. Investing such a significant proportion of fixed assets into an economy is simply done to keep the country's GDP numbers high. There are, however, a very few exceptions. A clear example: imagine a small island with a population of 10,000 people and a GDP of $200 million. One day a large oil reserve is discovered off the island's coast, and it will cost $400 million over four years to construct an operation to extract that oil from the sea floor. Essentially, this island is constructing infrastructure to generate long-term revenue for the island. But over four years, at least 33% of its GDP will be fixed investments.

The Bubble

In China, the majority of new property developments are generating new revenue for the developers, but those who purchase a dwelling from the developers are not. Why? In China it is common to purchase an investment property based on the speculation that the valuation of the property will continue to increase faster than any other form of investment on top of the rate of inflation. In China, it is also a common belief that if you buy an apartment in a new development, it should be kept in impeccable condition in order to attract the highest price when the buyer decides to sell (flip) the apartment to another buyer. For this specific reason, the typical Chinese property investor will not rent the property he or she has invested in. Hence, the world's biggest construction boom in history attracts no yield.

In these empty cities and busier cities, the majority of the properties are purchased at a significantly higher multiple versus income than in any Western country. If a Sydneysider thinks paying 9x his income for a standard property is high, wait till you see what the Chinese are paying for real estate relative to their incomes. New homes in China will generally cost anywhere from 15x to 40x the average annual income within a particular jurisdiction. To put it into perspective, let's look at the city of Taishan. About 1 million people live in and around the city, which is built to hold about 3 million people. Average annual income is somewhere between $7,000 to $9,000 per year, but the cost per square foot of real estate is about the same as it is in Houston, where the average income is around 7x to 8x higher. Is this confusing? It is to me. I have no clue as to where the average worker is getting money to buy an apartment in most Chinese cities (empty or full). Yes, there are a lot of wealthy individuals in China who can afford to buy 100 properties, but how is the average worker expected to live the new Chinese dream of homeownership? Somehow, a lot of them are living it. The biggest banks in China will not lend money to someone who wants to buy a property worth 20x more than their annual income. So, how are so many Chinese finding the money to buy property? They are using every cent saved by three generations of family wealth, or they're going through the shadow banking system— or they're doing a combination of both.

The name of the game in Chinese real estate is capital gain. The strategy is to buy a property at the current market rate, and before you know it, the value of the property will increase every month. A Guangzhou cab driver once told me, "Buy today, tomorrow price much higher." He definitely reminded me of the NYC and London cab drivers offering me free financial advice in 2006. But that's what the Chinese perceive their reality to be. If you can get in the property game you "will win." Because in China the belief is that property prices never go down. Only up!

So what happens if one day the property prices start to fall right across China? Let me be frank. China has probably built enough infrastructure to last at least the next fifteen to twenty-five years. Apart from a blatantly necessary handful of new roads in some of its congested cities, what more does China need? Since the mid-1990s, China has built 100 new airports with seventy more to be built over the next three years. Most of these airports operate fewer than three flights a day. They already have built an impressive high-speed rail network that is underutilized, and only a handful of key cities still need to be connected. There are unused stadiums in cities. But most importantly, China has probably constructed more residential and commercial real estate than it might ever need.

In my opinion, China has simply lost touch with reality. Why? Because when a new city is built in China, the intentions are wrong. They build cities to stimulate GDP growth by construction. If China's economy is to grow each year, construction has to grow more than it did the year before to offset the other sectors of the economy that are not growing as fast. That's the reason there is so much construction and what I believe to be simply wasteful spending in China. But in the name of China's GDP growth strategy, it has to be done.

This sentence comes straight from the Chinese National Bureau of Statistics website in 2014:

> "In the first eleven months, the floor space under construction by the real estate development enterprises accounted for 6,460.96 million square meters, up by 16.1% year-on-year, increased 1.5 percentage points over that in the first ten months. Of which, the floor space of residential building construction area was 4,729.41 million square meters, up by 13.5%."

For the numerically challenged, from January to November of 2013, in just eleven months, there was 6.4 billion square meters of real estate being constructed. Of that, 4.7 billion square meters was for residential space. In the first eleven months of 2013, China constructed 4.7 square meters of real estate for every man, woman and child in that country, or 3.45 square meters per person of residential real estate. That equates to a lot of Australian Iron Ore.

It was estimated that by 2010 there were up to 64 million vacant apartments in China—enough to house roughly 230 million people. If that statistic doesn't blow your mind, just imagine how many apartments are vacant today? It can only be a higher number.

China has set a goal to have 70% of its population urbanized by 2035. In 2012, roughly 52% of China's population of 1.36 billion was urbanized. To achieve 70% urbanization, 233 million people must move from the countryside to the cities. At this particular point in time, in 2014, there is an extremely good chance that there is today already enough vacant housing developed to house the extra 233 million people. What I'm trying to say is that there is already enough residential space built in urbanized areas to house 70% of the population—and whatever residential space China constructs from now on is excess space.

So, will there be that much more residential and commercial construction in China? Yes. Why? To stimulate GDP. As for population growth, it stands at just 0.5% per year. Not high enough to compensate for the extra residential space. In essence, China has already built all the residential property it will require until 2035. It's a big problem when you spend 48% of your GDP in fixed investments and you've already built all the residential property you need which makes up approximately half of the fixed investment.

Today, the average residential dwelling size in China is approximately 60 square meters. If China builds 4.7 billion square meters of residential real estate, that equals 78 million dwellings in just one year. With an average 3.1 persons per household in China, that is enough to house 242 million people, or 17% of the population. One way or another, until the brakes are put on fixed investment in China, there will be a new apartment or dwelling built for every man, woman and child in China between 2013 and 2021. How can that make sense to anyone?

If the growth trend continues, it is a clear indication of how ridiculous this residential construction boom is:

1) If China demolished all of its pre-2013 residential dwellings, it will build enough housing

stock to house all Chinese in just 4.3 years (according to 60m2 average dwelling size and 3.1 people per household)

2) If China demolishes all its pre-2013 residential dwellings and the average new dwelling size doubles to 120m2, the country will build enough housing to house the entire population in just 7.2 years.

Now just think what will inevitably have to happen to house price to income ratios in China once there is the realization that there may be more apartments in China than people. Even if the data released by the China Statistical Bureau is exaggerated, or under-exaggerated, it still displays the true scale of the over-construction that is happening in China.

What interests me is this: How can China navigate its way out of building a residential dwelling for every man, woman and child before 2021? There is only one way—by stopping construction. But this would come at an economic cost that will certainly put China into a depression. Why? Because fixed investments as a proportion of GDP in China is enormous. Regardless of how or why construction stops in China, the rest of the economy has absolutely no chance in covering the shortfall of any decrease in construction volume. The moment construction slows in China is the moment that the emerging world and Western countries that are dependent on China's economy—such as Australia—crumble.

In my opinion, when this realization finally kicks in, it will be the greatest property collapse in human history, and it will take down every country that has had any dependency on the Chinese economy. Whatever causes the China property bubble to pop, one thing is very clear: China cannot build its way out of this problem. It cannot build more infrastructure on top of the existing infrastructure, and more housing that simply won't ever be used. China would have to make a dramatic shift to change its economic model to support employment, income and enterprise beyond such dependency on construction. When the bubble eventually bursts in China, to stop its economy from sliding by up to 50% of today's GDP, it will have to find a new way to invest money into its economy. A significant transition will have to be made from construction of property to something else. Off the top of my head, the only way I can see the Chinese spending trillions elsewhere would be to fix their environment. Now, in my opinion that would not be a bad thing. It would be great for the future generations of Chinese to enjoy and appreciate the beautiful country that it is without the levels of toxic pollution that hang over the skies of China today. What an incredible sight that would be. Unfortunately, for Australia, clean technology is not exactly its forte when compared to iron ore production.

It's no secret that Australia and its politicians have placed a huge bet on the continuous economic growth of China. Almost all the financial assumptions made by government and the RBA assume Chinese growth to remain above 6.5% for years to come. Clearly, there is a limit as to how much more construction China can do before it makes its current situation worse than it already is. Of all the possible ways to trigger an economic downturn in Australia, an economic slowdown in China will create the biggest and fastest shock to the Australian economy.

It will create a powerful domino effect that aims directly at the second pillar of the Australian economy, which will in turn give a knockout blow to Pillars One and Three.

Chapter Six

The Second Pillar: Natural Resources

The backbone of the Australian economy

The natural resources industry—particularly, the mining industry—is the backbone of the Australian economy. Year after year, Australian mining companies are exporting a colossal amount of iron ore, and other raw goods such as coal and copper. The mining industry and companies such as Rio Tinto and BHP have also profited significantly from the rapid and recent (< fifteen years) economic development in China. The most essential ingredient that China needs to stimulate its GDP via way of construction is iron ore. Under the surface of Australia there is probably more iron ore than the world will ever need. But in recent times, mining companies have been relentlessly doing their very best to extract as much of that iron ore as possible to fuel China's incredible thirst to stimulate GDP. Over the last decade, hundreds of billions in local and foreign direct investment has made its way into the second pillar of the Australian economy to allow mining companies to significantly increase the volume of iron ore they are able to extract from the ground so they are able to meet demand from China. Essentially, the Australian mining industry has experienced a prolonged boom that has made it one of the largest industries in Australia. By market capitalization, it is the second largest industry only after the first pillar (financial services) of the Australian economy.

Western Australia (WA) has been the biggest beneficiary of the mining boom. Why? The majority of mining operations currently take place in WA. Mining has done absolute wonders for the WA economy. For years unemployment has remained low, incomes have increased, and a wealth of infrastructure has been built to accommodate the rapid growth of the mining sector.

Over the last fifteen years, the mining industry has not only benefited from increased demand of iron ore and other raw metals, but from a sharp increase in the traded spot price of commodities. Double jackpot! The spot price of iron ore back in August 2001 was $12.99 per metric ton. In April 2011, the spot price for iron ore peaked at $179 per metric ton. Since then the spot price has pulled back to a September 2012 low of $99 and then surged back to December 2013's price of $135 per metric ton. There are very few industries in the world that have a fifteen-times price increase on a product in the space of just ten years. The mining industry did, and it has profited significantly from the sharp increase in the spot price of iron ore and other natural resources.

Some of Australia's largest mining giants, such as BHP Biliton and Rio Tinto, are today among the largest companies in the world by market capitalization. In early 2013, BHP had a market capitalization of $205 billion. Rio Tinto, Australia's largest supplier of iron ore, had a market capitalization of $124 billion. These are two big mining and corporate giants. They dwarf the other Australian suppliers of iron ore. Fortescue Metals, for example, has a market capitalization of just $17.62 billion. When you start to dive deep into the financials of these three mining giants, you begin to understand the volume of risk they have taken in order to meet the China's ravenous demand for mined metals. Furthermore, when you look at the financial performance of these companies over the last fifteen years, and you break down the numbers, it is simply staggering how the mining industry has evolved to the position it is in today. Of all the industries I can think of, there is no industry in Australia that has transformed so quickly. Why? Because there is a country called China that has transformed just as quickly, and in order to be able to grow so fast, that country required anything resourceful that lied beneath the surface of Australia.

The rapid change of the mining industry (Cost vs. Sales)

Cost vs. sales calculates the amount of sales in dollar terms vs. the actual cost of sales. If we look back at August 2001, the spot price for a metric ton of iron ore was around $13. In 2001, Rio Tinto made an annual net profit of $1.079 billion against $10.438 billion of cost. What does this tell you? It tells you that it was costing less for Rio Tinto to extract a ton of natural resources (primarily iron ore) from the ground than the amount the company was able to get for that ton of product. The company essentially had a net profit margin of around 10%. This is a pretty good profit margin for such a big company after factoring in general deductions versus its positive cash flow.

This clearly illustrates that Rio Tinto was able to profit rather significantly from selling a metric ton of iron ore for $13. Fast-forward eleven years to 2012, and the differences are significant. By 2012, it cost Rio Tinto $75 to extract each metric ton of iron ore which it then turned around and sold for an weighted average price of $122.

Between 2001 and 2012, the cost for Rio Tinto to extract a single metric ton of iron ore rose from roughly $11 per metric ton to $75. This is an enormous change, and scary at first sight—but to a certain point, it is justified. Why? Because it is capital intensive to increase mining operations. To annually extract hundreds of millions of extra tons of iron ore from the ground, a lot more is required than just a shovel. An entirely new infrastructure system needs to be built to streamline the entire operational process—from the hole in the ground to the point where the iron ore goes onto a ship bound for China. Furthermore, more people are needed to manage and operate a significantly larger mining operation. When you conduct operations that are in the middle of a desert thousands of kilometers from the nearest major city, you need to find a way to attract workers to live in one of the harshest environments on planet Earth. How do you attract an individual who lives by the beach to work in a mine in the grueling heat? You have to pay them more than you would like—no one wants to leave the beach lifestyle to go and work in a mine in northwest Australia for minimum wage.

In a country like Australia, the larger the operation in an undesirable location, the higher the price you absolutely must pay for talent. When you suddenly need 30,000 workers in a country of just 23 million citizens who for the most part value a certain beach-oriented lifestyle, it's a struggle to find the appropriate manpower. Furthermore, the expertise to execute a rapid growth strategy with minimal complications also complicates matters. Essentially, you end up with a shortage of the human resources required to fulfill the mission. As for Rio Tinto and its rivals such as BHP and Fortescue, the market forced them to pay a very high price for human power to maintain their high-growth strategies. In a nutshell: the rate of Australian unemployment has remained very low over the mining sector's growth-spurt period.

It is understandable why it now costs $65 more to extract each metric ton of iron ore, but this is where it gets scary. Today, the cost to extract a metric ton of iron ore from the ground is high by historical standards relative to the long-term sale price of iron ore. The long-term historic average sale price is somewhere from $10 to $20 per metric ton. Hypothetically, if the spot price of iron ore returned tomorrow to its historic levels of $20 or less, Rio Tinto would make a loss of at least $55 per metric ton or greater. Why would such a drop in the spot price of iron ore occur? A drop in physical demand. And if Rio Tinto extracts less iron ore due to declining demand, the extraction cost becomes higher.

Like other mining companies, upon the eventual discontinuation of benchmark pricing, the price of natural resources that Rio Tinto supply to the open market became a traded commodity. Speculation can drive the price of key resources, such as iron ore, higher and lower. As experienced in 2008 during the height of the GFC, when demand for iron ore dried up for a short period of time, Rio felt the full brunt of a shock to the system. This shock, in turn, created high volatility within the natural resources sector. Rio Tinto's stock price declined by over 80% over the same period in 2008, with mounting fear that the company could possibly face bankruptcy.

Although Rio Tinto was not the only mining company with a cash-flow problem in 2008, it was the biggest of the mining companies that were on the chopping block. And the company was quickly running out of cash, as its growth-related capital-intensive investments required a significant amount of leverage to be acquired. At a certain point in 2008, Rio Tinto, Australia's largest producer of iron ore, had less than fourteen weeks of cash supply. Then China launched its stimulus package.

When China launched its stimulus, Rio and other mining companies were catapulted back into the game and given the green light to build an incredibly large-scale Australian mining operation. Rio Tinto is the biggest contributor of increasing production, with the objective to extract and sell 360 million metric tons of iron ore per year by 2015. That's roughly a 50% increase in output as compared to 2012.

Using Rio Tinto as a benchmark helps us to gain clearer insight into the financial health of other mining companies such as BHP Biliton and Fortescue Metals. And how are Rio Tinto's competitors faring? As long as the spot price of iron ore remains several percentage points above the companies' break-even points, they will remain profitable and continue to operate. However, if the spot price of iron ore passes below or remains only slightly above their break-even points, some of Rio Tinto's competitors may feel the pinch before Rio Tinto and its main rival, BHP, do. An example of this occurred in late 2012, when Fortescue Metals made swift efforts to restructure its debt obligations in order to protect the company from weakening iron ore spot prices. It was critical for Fortescue Metals to lower its repayment obligations to help reduce its break-even point.

The major difference among industry participants is the level of debt that needs to be serviced. On average, all industry participants—including Rio Tinto—hold large sums of debt. From a financial standpoint, all miners have fairly similar operating structures, clearly suggesting that there is no "absolutely significant" difference in the operational and financial structure that separates one miner from another. For example, the cost to extract each metric ton of iron ore does vary from one mining company to another (from USD$66 to $95 per metric ton). As long as the spot price of iron ore remains above $100 per metric ton and the momentum of commodity-based currencies continues to decline, the industry participants will remain profitable. However, Australian industry participants, including Rio Tinto and two of its competitors (BHP and Fortescue), have not had the luxury of weak Australian dollar, which has affected the cost of doing business in $USD terms. For comparison's sake, industry participants in Brazil and South Africa have benefited from the decline of their local currencies versus the $USD since the 2011 peak of the spot price. With the over-30% currency drops in South Africa and Brazil, South African and Brazilian industry participants have benefited from this buffer of lower costs of doing business in $USD terms to produce and sell a $USD-priced commodity. However, in Australia it has only been more recently that the Australian dollar has made a decline significant enough to make a positive impact to the sale price of iron ore in $AUD.

When a smaller mining company such as Fortescue Metals is analyzed and compared to the larger BHP or Rio Tinto, one senses key differences. Levels of debt in percentage terms that smaller iron ore miners (such as Fortescue Metals) must service compared to larger competitors are generally much higher and increase their risk profiles. This outlines the clear difference between the larger and more established mining giants and their smaller competitors. The financials and debt ratios of Rio Tinto look quite similar to those of BHP when compared to Fortescue Metals. For example, Fortescue Metals has more than double the debt versus equity compared to both of its larger rivals.

In good times, it is clear that the profit ratios of Fortescue Metals are more attractive than those of Rio Tinto and BHP. But when the industry environment becomes more challenging and the spot price of iron ore declines to near or below $100 per metric ton, the smaller company becomes more susceptible and vulnerable to the economic challenges. This is reflected in Fortescue Metals' stock price. When times are good and the spot price of iron ore rises, the stock value increases more in percentage terms than the stock values of BHP or Rio Tinto. When the spot price of iron ore declines, the stock price of Fortescue Metals declines much more rapidly than the stock prices of BHP and Rio Tinto. This suggests that Fortescue and other smaller mining companies that follow suit hold more risk than do their larger competitors. As an example, on a day when data suggests there will be less demand for iron ore, the stock price of Fortescue Metals dropped 6.5% versus the much smaller 2% and 3% drops in market valuation of the larger BHP and Rio Tinto respectively. This suggests that Rio Tinto is slightly more vulnerable to volatility movements than BHP—but that is nothing when compared to the vulnerability of the smaller mining companies.

If the spot price of iron ore were to drop to below-break-even point for all industry participants, the majority of the participants would face severe financial hardships before Rio Tinto would. Most competitors in Australia have significantly larger debt ratios, which become much more challenging to service when they are not able to make a profit. On top of that, there are other rivals in other countries able to remain profitable with sub-$66-per-ton iron ore.

Rio Tinto and its rivals believe the world will require the extraction of a lot more iron ore. This is in light of a changing economic environment and potential underlying risks to the Chinese economy. Based on the available data, clear signals exist that Fortescue Metals is the most vulnerable large (third largest in Australia) industry participant. Although the accounting practices make it more difficult to evaluate the exact cost to extract and sell a metric ton of iron ore, calculations suggest that it costs Fortescue somewhere between $84 to $90 per metric ton as compared to Rio Tinto's $75 and BHP's $70. Furthermore, Fortescue carries much more debt as a percentage of equity and assets. Fortescue is clearly the most vulnerable to a drop in the spot price of iron ore, with its higher levels of debt and cost of doing business its Achilles heel.

Macroeconomic forces that shape the mining industry

For the mining industry, macroeconomic forces can be defined as political, ecological, social, technological and economical drivers that shape the mining industry. In the last decade, the rise of the Chinese economy and its hunger to construct buildings and infrastructure clearly created a powerful opportunity within the mining industry. The Chinese construction boom led the financial markets to believe that companies that supply iron ore would continue to grow in the foreseeable future. This belief pushed the spot price of iron ore to historically high levels. Another key macroeconomic force that has helped shape the spot price of iron ore is the quantitative easing that was undertaken by major economies such as the United States, certain European countries, and Japan. Correlation between announcements of further quantitative easing by the former U.S. Federal Reserve chairman, Ben Bernanke, and the sharp spike in commodity prices was clear during the rebound of the financial markets from their 2008-09 lows. Although quantitative easing continues today, the momentum and market focus has now shifted; gold, copper and iron ore spot prices have faced headwinds in light of weakening Chinese economic data and the intention of the U.S. Federal Reserve to wind down quantitative easing measures.

When benchmarking the cost of extracting each ton of iron ore, Australian miners have the highest costs structure versus other key international iron ore mining operations. Australia was barely affected in the global financial crisis, hence, no drop in the high cost of labor or services.

The U.S. and Europe were once the largest global customers of natural resources. Today, they lack the comparable investment into infrastructure and construction compared to their Asian counterparts, particularly China. There is strong indication that the U.S. or European markets will not participate in heavy infrastructure spending while the cost of natural resources remains historically high. To put it into perspective, the United States has not built a new major airport since the mid 1990s. How many airports have been built in China over the same time? Over 100 airports with 70 more on the way.

Industry dependency on China

It's no secret that practically all mining-industry participants are dependent on China to continue to demand increasingly higher volumes of iron ore. Beyond any other macroeconomic factor, Rio Tinto, BHP, Fortescue Metals, and other major iron ore producers will face very stiff headwinds if the Chinese construction boom starts to recede. The scale of this construction boom is clearly visible in Chapter Five. No country in recorded human history has ever invested so much into construction as China has in the last fifteen years.

Based on statistical evidence in Chapter Five, I strongly believe that the mining industry is in for a shock. When an industry invests and leverages hundreds of billions into scaling up operations, it does so for the very long-term. You do not make a

$50 billion investment and expect to recoup the investment through sales within a five-year time frame. You must look well into the future and assess future demand. In this case, the mining industry has made a huge error. They have not done the proper mathematics to quantify precisely how much iron ore the world will need over the next twenty years; they have assessed how much iron ore the world will need for the next five years. On the basis of over a decade of highly accelerated growth, miners believe the long-term growth trend will only go higher.

My question to the second pillar of the Australian economy is this: Are you prepared for the possibility that twelve months from now some very powerful and influential individual in China is going to realize that if he keeps building homes as fast as he is, there will be more dwellings than people by 2021? Judging by the hundreds of billions that has been invested in the last several years to extract more iron ore than ever before, the answer is clearly "No." Let me be clear; there is no iron ore producer in Australia that can extract iron ore out of the ground for less than $66 per metric ton. When the construction boom in China ends (or shows the slightest hint of ending for whatever reason), the spot price of iron ore will drop significantly lower than $66 per metric ton. Furthermore, the Australian mining industry, alongside its global rivals, will be left with an incredible amount of leverage to pay back to creditors. This would be a catastrophic event.

In a nutshell, when 50% of Chinese demand for iron ore disappears, it will create an excess supply of iron ore by 25% to 40%. Sooner rather than later, the scale of construction in China has to slow, and fixed investments make up 48% of the Chinese economy. Other major importers of iron ore, such as Japan and Korea, only import a fraction of the amount of iron ore that China does. Even if they doubled their annual intake of iron ore, it would not be enough to cover the shortfall of demand.

To be caught in a period of demand destruction is catastrophic for a mining company. There is simply no possible way for all of the Australian mining companies to survive such an event. When China stops its hunger for iron ore, the iron ore companies will start to fall one by one as the spot price of iron ore will pass through their extraction costs per metric ton. One mining giant will fall after the other. Even Rio Tinto and BHP will struggle to survive.

Capital-intensive companies in any industry take more time to wind down operations when adapting to a new economic environment. Additionally, time is needed to sell off and ship the excess stock in a slowdown. For example, let's say that there are 10 million tons of iron ore en route to China from Australia at any given time, and for the last 10 years, 100% of that iron ore has been consumed. Now, if tomorrow there was only demand for 4 million tons of the iron ore already en route, there would be 6 million metric tons of excess supply, while the mining companies would be preparing to pump out another 10 million tons of iron ore. It would take months, a lot of pain, and, worst of all, a lot of bankruptcies in the mining industry for that process to rectify according to demand.

When this scenario becomes reality, it will send a shock to the Australian economy that has never before been seen. Australia has become extraordinarily dependent on the mining companies to maintain trade surpluses. When exports of iron ore come to a near halt in a wasteful attempt to revive the spot price of iron ore, it will send the $AUD crashing. At that particular point in time, whether the $AUD is trading at .90c, .80c, or even .60c against the $USD, the $AUD will take a significant dive, and the domino effect will drive the Australian economy into unchartered waters that will inevitably sink the Australian economy. Why? Because there is no mining company in Australia today able to extract a metric ton of iron ore for less than the historical sale price.

When the mining giants begin to drop like flies, the Australian government will not be able to bail out the industry. This is because the world may not require today's demand for iron ore and other natural resources for the next twenty to twenty-five years. To subsidize such a large proportion of national income would cost the Australian government $55 per metric ton. Multiply that by several hundred million tons, and hundreds of billions of dollars of printed money would be simply wasted to save an industry that did not make an accurate forecast regarding demand of its product. Wasted because if iron ore is at $20 a metric ton, it's not even enough to cover debt repayments to the mining industry's creditors, let alone all the other costs such as wages, maintenance, and operational costs alongside under-utilized expensive infrastructure.

The natural resources industry in Australia is the pillar that is affected the most directly by indirect consequences offshore. There's not much the Australian government can do to convince other countries and their buyers of natural resources to buy more volume than they need. Quantitative easing in the United States, which benefited the spot price of iron ore, is now undergoing the anticipated tapering process. How continuous tapering will impact the spot price of iron ore is inconclusive. The last thing on the mind of the U.S. Federal Reserve is the wellbeing of the Australian mining industry.

The industry participants of the second pillar of the Australian economy better hope that China is actually crazy enough to knock down every building it has ever constructed in the past ten years to pave way for a new construction projects. Unfortunately for the second pillar, there is very little chance of that happening.

The Second Pillar hopes that Pillars One and Three fail before it does

After the tough picture I have just painted of mining industry's fate, there is a chance—although very small—that a domestic implosion of the Australian economy might benefit Pillar Two. This benefit wouldn't last forever, but it would extend at least to the point where it buys the industry time to make the critical adjustments necessary to soften the pain of a Chinese economic slowdown. How would this happen? A domestic economic slowdown that affects Pillars One and Three, alongside continued expansion of iron ore demand from China.

If the Chinese continue with the objective to build a residential dwelling for every man, woman and child while the domestic economy of Australia has internally imploded, the value of the $AUD will be brought down versus the $USD. If Pillars One and Three struggle to interact like they have for the last several years on the back of increased unemployment, the domestic economy will go into recession. This will suck the life out of the $AUD. In the meantime, China will still be purchasing iron ore at a premium $USD spot price. The cost to extract a metric ton of iron ore in $USD terms will decline significantly. For example, if it costs a mining company AUD$90 and the Aussie currency falls to 0.50c against the $USD, the cost in $USD for the mining company drops down to $45 per metric ton. This buys the second pillar time, and increases the possibility that its participants can build their balance sheets with cash and pay down a greater proportion of debt that was acquired through the aggressive expansion stage.

Although the chance of the Australian economy having an internal implosion is slim, it remains a plausible prospect. The domestic demise of the Australian economy is the second pillar's best hope of staying alive just that much longer. If, during this phase of opportunity, the industry is still profiting from Chinese demand, it will be at this point that the industry as a whole will need to take advantage of the moment and make every effort possible to reduce its credit exposure and prepare to batten down the hatches. This would be achieved by taking advantage of a weak domestic economy and increasing willingness among job hunters to work for less pay at mine sites. It would take years for the mining industry to prepare itself for the reality of $20 per metric ton of iron ore. In this scenario, there is a slight chance that a handful of mining giants could survive a following economic downturn, based on the notion that some are better able to bring down their debt exposures.

Internal politics

Anyone who works for an organization and is trying to work his or her way up the ladder knows that internal politics gets in the way of an organization's productivity. There is employee competition that extends all the way down to being assigned the parking spot closest to the office entrance. Mining companies are no different. These corporations have highly talented executives managing exceedingly complex cross-border businesses. I would like to know this: when a large company does its forecasting for the long term (ten to twenty years), at what probability do the executives assume there will be no interrupted growth over this period? Yes, I understand that it is human nature to ride out the good times for as long as possible. It's like that the mining industry executives learned nothing when analyzing the 2008 damage caused to financial institutions in the northern hemisphere. As much as Australia's banks and households are overleveraged, the mining industry has exposure not only to debt, but also to a product that is traded. What Chinese government data do they use to measure future prospects? Have any employees of these mining giants stood up and said that something is not right here? Or do they get fired for offering diverse and credible views that suggest the mining boom may end?

In my consulting days I always kept my own professional promise to myself: "Always speak your mind in a constructive manner backed up by data!" It is in this way that you look out for your clients. They depend on you to deliver substantive, data-supported strategies that make them well aware of the risks when going for growth. But this tactic doesn't always work out as well as you would like. I was always known to be the consultant with the diverse view. I refused to be the consultant who always told the clients what they wanted to hear. I was more concerned about what it was that the client absolutely had to hear. I was always willing to be kicked off a project in the name of doing my utmost to offer the best service and uphold my professional dignity. It's ok as a consultant to challenge the clients and broaden their views on possible risks for particular projects. When you look at something in a different way, you are able to offer diversity. When everyone thinks alike, mistakes and misjudgments are made. While a leader of a multinational organization is trying to power through one milestone after another without looking left or right, mistakes are made. When CEOs of publically traded companies are more concerned about short-term benefit for investors versus long-term gain, mistakes are made.

When I look at the mining industry, there has to be a CEO or high-level manager of one of these organizations in Australia who has done the math and realized the direction China is heading. Like the executives of Pillar One, the management teams at Australia's mining giants chose to go for growth at the risk of adopting an unsustainable business model. In the last ten years, the natural resources sector (in Australia and worldwide) had a golden opportunity to influence Chinese growth. Moderating the increase of production would have proactively moderated Chinese growth. In return, mining companies would have had a sustainable business model that would have lasted a lot longer than the current strategy of going for growth, in addition to lower output costs and a quarter century of $120+ for each and every metric ton of iron ore. Now it's too late.

Chapter Seven

The Third Pillar: Real Estate

Property Only Goes Up . . . Until it Comes Crashing Down

The Australian real estate industry. Where do I start? Relative to the size of the Australian economy this industry is huge. Everyone from homebuyers, property investors, renters, real estate agents, builders, plumbers, gardeners, insurance companies and pundits make up this industry. And let's not forget the good people from the first pillar of the Australian economy that lend money to every aspect of this industry.

It is almost impossible to attend a gathering in Australia—whether it be with friends, business associates, or the person sitting next to you on the plane—and not talk about real estate. After returning to Australia with the intention of permanently residing here, I cannot help but see how caught up everyone is in real estate. One way or another, everyone is involved in the industry as a potential buyer, a professional industry participant or a long/short-term investor. "Lindsay! Property only goes up in Australia!" If I was paid a dollar for every time someone said this to me. . . . Not only is real estate the most discussed topic among Australians, they are incredibly passionate about it. Real estate has become The National Sport that can be played at almost any age.

Reading the Sydney Morning Herald's property section, I feel like I've returned to a city full of billionaires! I've never been to a city where the majority of the residents talk about a million dollars like it's going out of fashion. "Apartment sells for $1.235 million above reserve," Stephen Nicholls headlines. It's like central Sydney is on a mission to boast higher property prices than those in Mayfair, London! What about the rest of Sydney? My friends tell me all the time, "Lindsay, a million dollars is nothing in Sydney!" I thought London was property mad. When you come to Sydney, the Londoners look tame! You'd think that the majority of Australians have a PhD in Property Prices Only Go Up! How did Australians become so addicted to property?

In the last few years, Australia has become more known for being an expensive place to live. But what most blows the minds of visitors to Australia is the cost of property and living. A successful American entrepreneur I know lives in Bondi Beach. He has come to the conclusion that everyone in Sydney has to be a drug dealer in order to spend as much as they do on property and entertainment. Anyone I meet abroad who has visited Australia in recent years always asks me the exact same question: "Why is Australia so expensive, and why are property prices so ridiculous?" I just shake my head: "It's one big bubble." But ask most Australians who haven't lived overseas the same questions, and they will give you the all-too-familiar answer that sends shivers down the spine of any neutral analyst who has no interest in whether the Australian property market rises or falls.

Two magic words. Why are property prices so high in Australia? "Because," they say, **"it's different."**

It's Different

I can't emphasize enough how Australians really do believe that Australian life and property prices are higher because Australia is different to every other place on the planet. But before I get started, I want to tell you a story about a famous diaper company that wasted millions of dollars on research because their Japanese executives wanted to design a new diaper for Japanese babies. Yes, you guessed right—the Japanese executives really believed that Japanese babies were "different." After the parent company paid a consulting company millions of dollars to undertake a vast amount of research, the final conclusion came as a shock to the Japanese executives of this diaper company: "Japanese babies crap. And that they crap just like any baby, regardless of nation."

When it comes to real estate, the Japanese learned the world's biggest lesson about thinking they were "different." Between 1986 and 1991, they thought the law of economics could not affect them because they were "different." By 1991, they realized that the law of economics cannot be defied. The Japanese property bubble burst, and it has never recovered. The Irish, the Spaniards and the Americans all know what it's like to be "different." That "D" word is an incredibly dangerous word when it comes to defending the high price of property when the "B" word is supported by history generally having a good track record of repeating itself when an industry attempts to defy the law of economics.

I agree that the property market in Australia is different—but not for the same reasons that most Australians would. The real estate pundits can't emphasize enough how different the Australian property market is to those of other nations. These are very powerful people in the Australian public eye. You have the Australian Treasurer, Joe Hockey, telling Americans on CNBC that they don't understand the Australian property market—that it's a "different asset class." He says, "A lot of commentators particularly over here [the U.S.] don't understand the Australian housing market." After telling the Americans that they're clueless, he marches on: "Australians have the largest homes in the Western world, so it's a very different asset class in Australia versus other jurisdictions."

If only Mr. Hockey had done just the tiniest amount of research before he made that comment. In fact, Mr. Hockey, the average American dwelling is actually larger than the average Australian dwelling. Big mistake. But at least we know Mr. Hockey is human—he makes mistakes! Then again, would the Australian Treasurer ever go live on American television to say, "It's a bubble!" Australian property prices are going to take the biggest nosedive and Australia is going to plunge into recession—so DON'T INVEST IN AUSTRALIA!" Do that as Treasurer, and you are committing political suicide.

Famed American demographer and fairly accurate predictor of bubbles popping Harry Dent made a visit to Australia in February of 2014. Dent predicts that Australian property prices will fall by up to 50%. SMH reported his comments, and quoted Harry: "Bubbles always go up to the point where they just become unaffordable—and then they burst." SMH being the newspaper that it is then brings in its arsenal of pundit defenders of the Australian property market. None other than Dr. Andrew Wilson responded: "His prediction doesn't reflect either the history or the underlying strength of the Australian housing market's dynamics," said the senior economist at Australian Property Monitors (owned by Fairfax Media). "The preconditions are not there. There is no bubble to burst." And then SMH brings in another pundit who claims that Mr. Dent is, "scaremongering." Essentially what they are trying to tell Mr. Dent is that the property market in Australia is "different." Pundits will tell you time and time again that things are different here in Australia because demand outstrips supply. That, apparently, is the "difference." What the pundits always fail to mention is that demand in Australia is now 150% dependent on the banks' abilities to lend excessive amounts of debt to hopeful property buyers.

My opinion is based on "actual research," and I believe the Australian property market at this point in time is, in fact, "different." Why? Because the Australian property market may be in the midst of the biggest property bubble that has ever existed in the history of modern Western civilization. And that is different. Essentially, Australians have talked themselves into believing that property prices only go up, and they are leveraged through the roof to own their little piece of the Australian dream.

The insane cost of real estate in Australia

As a keen external observer of the Australian property market, I'm simply shocked at how high property prices have managed to climb. By value, Australian homebuyers and property investors are willing to pay more for a dwelling than are the homebuyers in any other Western nation. The Norwegians and the Swiss have higher average incomes than those of Australian households, and they pay less for their dwellings and overall land price per square meter than Australians do. And with that in mind, think about the fact that the Swiss are talking about a bubble in their property market. Yes, Australian homes are larger than the average Swiss or Norwegian dwelling, but Australia has much more land, and the cities by area are significantly larger and lack density.

Based on Demographia's annual International Housing Affordability Survey in late 2013, **median** property prices in Australian cities and regional towns range from $818,000 Port Hedland, WA (a town in the middle of nowhere that has a lot of iron ore) down to $213,000 in Mildura (a town of 31,000 inhabitants that lies 400 kilometers inland from Adelaide and 500 kilometers away from Melbourne— or, as an American would say, somewhere in the middle of BFN. In this price range lies the median property prices of the major cities: Sydney ($722,000) Melbourne ($595,000), Perth ($508,000), Brisbane ($442,100) and Adelaide ($392,000). And since Demographia published this data, home prices—particularly in Sydney and Melbourne—have increased approximately 10% in just a few short months.

Every Australian city and regional town, except for three, have a higher median cost of property than that of Chicago, Illinois (USD$209,000). Have you ever been to Chicago? The GDP of Chicago dwarfs that of any Australian city or state with over $500 billion in annual productivity. Can an Australian real estate pundit please explain to me why it costs about the same amount to buy a dwelling in Mildura (BFN) as it does in Chicago? Is there really a housing shortage in the middle of nowhere that justifies the same price be paid for a dwelling as the price paid for a dwelling located in the third-largest U.S. city? Surely there must be more people wishing to move to Chicago than to Mildura? I know I'm comparing apples and oranges here, but who the heck wouldn't in this case?

Can Australia have such overwhelming demand as to drive the average property price in a regional town such as Bendigo to AUD$315,000—6x the average Bendigo-household's income? Bendigo is a regional town surrounded by farmland with just over 80,000 residents in a 146-square-kilometer area. There is simply no shortage of land in and around Bendigo. How did Bendigo real estate become more expensive than the real estate of most major cities in the Western world outside of Australia? Whether you're examining one of the five major Australian cities, or the small regional hubs in the middle of farmland, one has to ask why housing affordability has soared out of reach of so many people but demand is so high? The real estate pundits have an answer to everything. "There is a housing shortage," is what Australians are being told. A housing shortage. When I think of a housing shortage, I think of people sleeping on the streets. Have the pundits scared Australians into actually thinking there is a housing shortage? Because when I look at the core data from the Australian Census Bureau, I see a completely different story. According to the census, in 2011 the Greater Bendigo area had 38,222 occupied dwellings and 3,897 unoccupied dwellings. Practically one home in every ten was unoccupied, and the story is similar in every Australian city and town. This 2011 census data shows a different story to the media-spread story of "the great Australian housing shortage of 2011." Nine percent of dwellings were unoccupied in Melbourne, 9.6% in Perth, 8.1% in Adelaide, 7.2% in Sydney, and 7.3% in Brisbane. Everywhere in Australia, you find a fairly similar story. Once again, why has the price of Australian real estate climbed so high? Aussie John from Aussie Home Loans will tell you, "it's all about supply and demand." But as previously mentioned, there is a lot more to it than just supply and demand. Australian financial institutions are willing to lend a greater amount of money to homebuyers than are the financial institutions in any other country in the Western world. As I said in Chapter Four, **In Australia, Real Estate prices do not depend on supply and demand, but the banks' willingness to lend excessively to property purchasers.**

Who is buying Australian real estate?

In the Western world, cities and smaller towns that are famous for their high property prices generally share the same characteristics in relation to purchasing eligibility. Monaco, London, New York and San Francisco have something in common. Anyone from anywhere can buy any desired residential property as long as they have the funds to do so. In Australia, the rules are very different. Yes— "different." Australia's foreign investment policy for residential real estate is very clear:

1) Non-resident foreign persons "cannot" buy **established** dwellings as investment properties or as homes.

2) Non-resident foreign persons have to apply to buy **new** dwellings in Australia. Such proposals are normally approved without conditions.

3) Non-resident foreign persons have to apply to buy vacant land for residential development. These proposals are normally approved subject to conditions (e.g., that ongoing construction begins within twenty-four months).

There has been a lot of talk about how the price of real estate is being driven up by non-resident foreigners coming to Australia and buying up real estate in major Australian cities. This is possible in relation to newly constructed homes and vacant land. But with only a very few exceptions, a non-resident cannot buy an existing dwelling. Australia is a multicultural society and interested buying parties who look and sound Chinese are probably either Australian residents or citizens. Journalists call them "foreign buyers." Unless it's a new dwelling or vacant land, the people who are buying property are Aussies. "Temporary residents" can only purchase new homes or a single existing home if they are going to live in that home, but they must sell the property when they leave Australia.

Yes, there are foreign buyers purchasing newly built houses and apartments, and land. Foreign buyers purchase approximately one in every eight (12.5%) newly constructed homes in Australia. Foreigners buy 75% of newly built homes in central London. It's a lot harder for wealthy foreign buyers to drive up the price of real estate in a particular jurisdiction if they are only purchasing 12.5% of newly built homes. The exception is if the bulk of the foreigners are significantly attracted to a particular neighborhood in a city. This is the case for just a handful of neighborhoods in the major world capitals where there is significant supply of new homes. Using London as an example, the Central London neighborhoods of Mayfair, Knightsbridge, St John's Wood, Kensington and Chelsea are the neighborhoods where the well-heeled foreigner seeks to buy a dwelling. If a property on the market is not in one of those neighborhoods, there is a good chance the cost of the dwelling per square meter is significantly lower—even if it's just a 10-minute drive away. It is extremely difficult for a local Brit to come up with more cash than a rich foreign buyer. On top of that, the entire London real estate market is open to foreigners, whether the dwellings are new or old.

So if foreign buyers purchase roughly 12.5% of the newly constructed Australian homes, who are the other 87.5% who are buying newly built homes? And who is buying all the existing dwellings in Australia? **Australians**. Yes, the rest of the residential real estate market is exclusively reserved for Australian citizens and permanent residents. Yes, each property market in Australia is "different"—but when you break down the demographics of the average property purchaser, you have five unique subsectors.

1) Property Investors (Landlords)

2) Property Developers

3) Climbing-the-Ladder Homeowners

4) Empty nesters and retirees

5) First-time Homeowners.

In Australia, the common belief is that you cannot go wrong if you invest in real estate. As part of an investment portfolio, it is not uncommon to seek an investment property with the aim of getting capital gain, and/or yield on your investment by renting out the dwelling to a tenant. Property investment is big business in Australia. Essentially, you have two clear subsectors for property investors. Investors/landlords seeking yield and investors seeking capital gain.

On one hand, you have the long-term-yield property investor: The landlord. Landlords generally seek to hold their investments for the long-term in order to receive consistent rental income. Long-term secure rental income is their priority. A landlord seeks long-term consistent revenue to potentially help secure his or her retirement, or as an alternative source of revenue during retirement. Unless retired, these individual investors generally have 9-to-5 jobs, or are business owners. They generate income from their places of employment on top of the rents received from any tenants who rent their investment properties.

On the other hand, you have property investors who seek capital gain. Essentially, this person wants to buy a house and sell it within a certain time frame at a significantly higher price than it was originally purchased for. Property investors primarily seeking capital gain will generally make resourceful modifications to the properties they purchase to increase value. These investors are commonly individuals or couples who spend their lives jumping and moving from one property to another in the pursuit of capital gain. Why? Because there is a tax loophole in Australia that reduces Capital Gains Tax

(CGT) exposure when selling an investment property. If you are an Australian property investor and you purchase a property and live in it for at least twelve months, the property is not subject to CGT. Like yield investors, there is a pretty good chance a property investor seeking capital gain has a full-time job outside of the property investment. However, the difference is that the property investor will generally make modifications to the investment property over a certain period of time in order to increase capital gain. Generally, twelve months after the property investor becomes a resident of his investment property, the individual or couple will put the property on the market and hopefully sell it at a significantly higher price than it was originally acquired for.

Property developers are in the business of constructing new dwellings for profit. This is their job. They generally seek to buy existing dwellings or vacant land at an attractive price. If there is an existing property on the land they purchase, they usually will demolish it and build a new dwelling to increase the potential sale value. It is not uncommon for Australian property developers to purchase several homes next to each other, demolish them, and build an apartment or townhouse complex. Property developers are generally more time sensitive than property investors are, as the longer it takes to sell a development, the more it costs. Time is money. To reduce risk and exposure to debt, property developers generally attempt to sell their newly constructed developments to buyers prior to completion. Large property developers in Australia have more complex operations and employ large pools of talent to conduct large-scale operations. Essentially, property developers seek to make

102

significant capital gain versus the overall investment into a particular project.

Climbing-the-ladder homeowners can generally be classified as those who own an existing dwelling, but seek to purchase a larger home. For example, a married couple who owns a small 2-bedroom apartment seeks to start and raise a family in a 4-bedroom house instead of their existing apartment. Generally, those who seek to climb the property ladder are not at retirement age and will usually continue to purchase properties that are larger than the property they own. Furthermore, unlike property investors seeking capital gain, they will usually make fewer improvements to their current place of residence. Like property investors seeking capital gain, climbing the ladder will attract the same CGT benefits.

Empty nesters and retirees who are scaling back generally seek to buy smaller homes than the family homes they inhabit which have become too large in the absence of children, or are physically too difficult to maintain. Empty nesters and retirees will generally seek to buy an apartment or townhouse that is more suitable for their lifestyle goals in the latter part of life, and costs significantly less than the sale price of their larger property. This will allow them to have more access to cash during the later stages of their lives.

First-time homebuyers are generally younger individuals and couples who either seek to buy or have purchased their first dwelling. First-homebuyers are generally required to spend several years saving the cash needed to make a fair deposit on a home. Before purchasing a home, first-time buyers are generally renting a property or are still living with their parents. For the current generations of young Australians, it is becoming increasingly common to remain under their parents' roofs until the age of 24 or even higher.

When you assess the different subsectors of real estate buyers, there are clear advantages for some subsectors versus others in relation to affordability. Who ends up buying a particular property versus other interested parties seeking the same dwelling? The person who pays the highest price. Who is the least likely to have access to a larger sum of funds? First-time homebuyers. Who is more likely to get access to debt? Those with a track record and a larger deposit. Who generally has little track record and a smaller deposit? First-time homebuyers. Which subsector is chronically priced out of the current market? First-time homebuyers.

First-time homeowners today have never made up such a small percentage of the property-purchasing population. By November 2013, the first-time homebuyer subsector made up less than 13% of new home-loan recipients. First-time homebuyers have also never taken such a small share of new home loans. Historically, they have taken at least 22% of the share of new home loans. That percentage has dropped by half.

When first-time homeowners are priced out of the market in what is known as a property boom, other buyers from different subsectors have to make up the shortfall to maintain high demand so that land and dwelling prices increase. And in this particular booming market environment, those selling have had no problems offloading their properties.

If first-time homebuyers are priced out of the market, who has the purchasing power? The other four subsectors—but most particularly, property investors seeking capital gain—have significantly increased their share of home loans and purchases. Why? Because interest rates in Australia are at historic lows and the banks are more than willing to lend exorbitant sums of money to investors seeking capital gain. The banks lent property investors $26.7 billion in November 2013—25% more than they loaned a year earlier. Low interest rates in Australia have sparked an incredible rush of property investors who want to take on high-risk interest-only repayment loans in pursuit of short-term capital gains. First-time homebuyers are also priced out of the market by empty nesters and retirees.

Essentially, you have three big subsectors (first-time buyers, empty nesters/retirees, and capital gain investors) of real estate buyers vying for real estate within a specific price range. In Sydney, this range is between $600,000 and $1 million. Property prices in Sydney are increasing at a faster pace than they are throughout the rest of the country. Within this price range, there are the bulk of first-time homebuyers on the lower end, (because properties that first-time homebuyers were seeking have now been priced just out of their general price range), and the other two subsectors (which are now in competition with each other). In a matter of months, the first-time homebuyer has been left behind to pick up the property below the median price. So, now they are vying with the landlords who are challenging each other for the smaller dwellings that tenants love to rent.

You now have the ladder climbers and a portion of investors buying the bulk of the $1 million to $1.3 million market. There are 800 suburbs that make up Sydney. It is common knowledge that one in every five suburbs in Sydney has a median property price of more than $1 million. Property developers cover the whole property market building everything from apartment complexes to luxury homes. Although they function at slightly lower overall property prices, cities and towns across Australia have similar dynamics.

When property prices don't make sense in relation to income, the market is probably in a bubble.

The populations of Sydney and Melbourne combined make up roughly 37% of the entire Australian population—and they both have the highest property-price-to-household-income ratios in the country. Before the recent spike in property prices, Sydney real estate had a median price-to-income ratio of 9.0x, and Melbourne's was 8.4x. Recent gains in property prices suggest that Sydney's price-to-income ratio is closer to the 10x-income range. Unless the circumstances are extraordinary, it is practically impossible for any property market to reach such a scale relative to household income levels without risky lending.

Let's put things into perspective, because this is truly insane. And, yes, I'm going to compare apples to oranges. The average loan in the state of New South Wales (NSW) is now greater than $500,000. When converted to $USD, the median house price in the New York metropolitan area is lower than the average amount of a home loan throughout the entire state of NSW. The average size of an NSW home loan is 2.7x the median house price in Houston. The first pillar generally demands a 20% deposit before it lends the remaining 80% in the form of debt. To get a more compelling illustration of the Australian property bubble, calculate the difference between the amount of new home mortgage obligations acquired versus median household income. For example, look at NSW with its average home loan of $507,000 versus a median household income of $66,280. NSW new home loans equate to 7.6x NSW income. That is a higher ratio than the property-price-to-household-income ratio in Spain at the absolute peak of the Spanish property bubble. So what's different? Australians homebuyers, by an incredible margin, are the largest home-loan borrowers in the world, not only by the amount of the loan, but relative to household income. If you borrow 7x the amount of your income to purchase a home, you have very little margin of error throughout the course of the binding financial agreement with the loaning bank.

Taking on excessive leverage is dangerous under any circumstance. But as they say: greater the risk, greater the reward. The residential property market in Australia clearly holds a significant amount of risk in the form of debt. When you hear Australian real estate and banking pundits say that Australian banks are responsible lenders, and that the European and American banks were lending recklessly before the GFC, you have to wonder if they've done their research. In my opinion, it is clear that they have not.

Real estate agents

The real estate industry employs a wealth of Australians. Real estate agencies generally offer potential employees an exciting and rewarding lifelong career in the marketplace. Being a real estate agent is a highly interactive role where communication and relationship-building skills are absolutely essential.

In Australia, a dwelling is generally offered to the open market by a real estate agent. Like investment bankers, agents generally work on a commission basis to broker the sale or rental of a property—and they work hard to attract a high level of interest in a particular property they are selling. Real estate agencies are private entities, and they are in the business to make a profit, just like any other business. The higher the price of a sold property, the higher the income the responsible real estate agent or agency will earn based on their standard commission rate. What's wrong with this? Nothing. Commission is their incentive and that is their job. Real estate agents have just as much interest in selling property at a high price as any other market-driven industry.

Real estate agents are regular commentators in the public eye. It is in their best interest to stimulate the market and attract buyers and sellers of real estate to their business. So you will never hear a real estate agent say, "Now is not a good time to buy property." It is not in the interest of the real estate industry to sell property at lower prices because they will earn less in valuable commissions. If a real estate agency charges 2% commission on the successful sale of a $1 million property versus a $300,000 property, the agency will earn $14,000 more in commission for selling the $1 million property. That's a big difference to an agent's profit margin and overall profitability.

Every neighborhood in Australia has a few more real estate agencies than it did a decade ago, and these agencies compete among each other to win the exclusive right to sell a vendor's property. On the back of twenty-five recession-free years, the real estate industry has grown significantly—and from the look of it, there seems to be enough business for all the real estate agents. When compared to other markets, the consistently high demand for property in Australia has meant that there has been little need to go out and find buyers. Trying to sell a property in a nosedive market can get tough for real estate agents. In the United States, Ireland, Spain and Japan, the real estate agents have experienced first-hand how challenging it is to sell a property during a severe economic downturn. In Las Vegas, there were roughly 17,500 real estate agents operating within the metropolitan area back in 2008. By 2013, there were just 11,300. That's close to a 36% decline in headcount. One way or another when the Australian economy faces the harsh reality that recessions can hit Australia, the real estate agencies will have to tighten their belts to weather what could be the toughest storm they have had to face. They will have to become accustomed to years of mediocre sales at much lower sale prices. Not every real estate agency can survive such a storm. On the flipside, the well-managed agencies that prepared for tough times will have a lot less competition in the future. At the end of the day, as with any industry, the brands that provide the best customer service, the best product for their customers, and the best deal closures at the most competitive pricing on behalf of their clients, are the brands that will probably ride out the storm. Real estate is about results, and it takes hard work to achieve these results in this industry.

Auctions

Taking a property to auction is a popular method of sale for a property in Sydney and Melbourne. I enjoy attending auctions; they're entertaining—especially the auctioneers. It's amazing how they tend to describe to the crowd the properties that they are selling. It can be the saddest looking 50-year-old 2-bedroom home that hasn't been renovated since 1971, but the auctioneer will transform it into a piece of art: "Ladies and gentlemen, welcome to the auction of this charming property full of potential in an exquisite location. It boasts two splendid bedrooms... blah, blah, blah." By the time the auctioneer has finished, you would think the saddest 2-bedroom property was Windsor Palace, were you blindfolded. And then it's down to business; the auction begins.

In the auctions I've attended, I've rarely seen a registered bidder rush to be the first to bid. The silence is momentarily uncomfortable, then the auctioneer will make a small joke to relax the crowd, and then someone finally makes the first bid. After that, it's off to the races with the first-time homebuyers: "$600,000" yells the first bidder. The auctioneer notes that the bid is really on the low side, "But let's start with $600,000 and see where it takes us." Three other young bidders jump in: "$610,000," "$620,000," "$640,000," "$650,000," "$660,000," "$680,000," "$690,000." In a matter of fifteen seconds the bidders have pushed the price up by $90k. In come the property-investor bidders: "$720,000." All heads turn to the person who just bid $30,000 higher. And it's Adios to the first-time buyers. The bidding continues with bidders ranging between the ages of forty and fifty-five. "$730,000," "$740,000," "$750,000," "$760,000," "$770,000." The auctioneer is having a field day: "GOOD BIDDING!" he says to the previous bidder. "$780,000," then "$800,000," "$810,000," "$825,000," "$830,000," "$840,000," Now we're down to just two bidders. "$850,000," "$855,000," "$860,000," "$870,000," "$875,000," "$880,000," "$882,000," "$885,000." The people are shaking their heads in disbelief; the two bidders start to slow in their bid making: "$887,000," "$889,000." The more confident-looking bidder raises his hand: "$891,000." There is a very long pause; the auctioneer adds pressure: "Can I get $895 from you, sir? Ladies and gentlemen, are we all done? Going once, going twice." The hand goes up: "$895,000," "$900,000," It's like people have seen a ghost: "$901,000," "$902,000," "$903,000," "$904,000," "$906,000," "$907,000." The tension is out of this world and neither bidder wants to look like the cheapskate, but they have their financial limits— which they probably past $80,000 ago. "$908,000," "$909,000," "$910,000." It hurts just to watch. "This is just insane," the woman standing behind me mutters. "$911,000," "$912,000," "Can I get a bid from you, sir" the auctioneer demands of one of the bidders. He then goes on: " Ok, ladies and gentlemen, for the third time, are we all done? Going once, going twice, going . . ." And the hand goes up! "$913,000," "$915,000." $2,000 more has been bid, this has got to send the other bidder into submission. But not so fast, he goes for it:

"'$916,000," "$916,500," "$917,500," "'$918,000," "$919,000," "$920,000," "$921,000," "$921,500," "Going once, going twice, sir, can you make another bid?" Unless you have seen an auction get to this point, you can't imagine the pressure of just being an observer. What the experience must feel like for these two bidders is unfathomable. They've put all their heart and emotion and debt into this. And then: "going, going . . . " "$922,000," "$922,500," "$923,000." One of the bidders can't stand still—he looks like he's going to have a heart attack; but just as the auctioneer is about to yell, "Sold!" "$923,500!" And immediately the confident bidder backs up with a whopping "$924,000!" Finally— finally!—the other bidder says, "You can have it, mate." He's out. "Going once, going twice . . . and sold!!"

If you are a regular observer of auctions in either Sydney or Melbourne, you have probably witnessed a similar auction. When just two interested buyers raise the price of a house by $74,000, you realize something important: It only takes two interested parties who are highly motivated and supported by a bank to dramatically increase the price of a property by a significant margin. This is how a property market can get out of control. Just two people. A reverse in property prices happens because the competition to purchase a particular property moves to just one or none.

As the price of real estate continues to rise in these cities, there has been a significant increase in the number of sellers putting their houses up for auction. It has become increasingly common to have over 1000 properties for auction in Melbourne on any given Saturday. Sydney has recently hit around the

700 mark. The auction is the moment when all the buyers come together to bid for a property. The property will generally be sold under the hammer to the highest bidder, unless the bidders fail to surpass the reserve price set by the vendor. Vendors are also allowed to make a single bid. Why would a vendor bid on his own house? Vendors will set a reserve price prior to the auction. Only the real estate agent and auctioneer will know what that reserve price is. Once the bidding passes the reserve price, the property will be sold. If the price comes in under the reserve price, the property may be "passed in" at the vendor's discretion. As vendors are allowed one bid, they make that bid very strategically. If it looks like bidders will hike the price above the reserve, the vendor will most probably not need to use the single bid. But if, for example, the reserve price is $900,000 and the auctioneer is challenged to get bidders to hit or pass the reserve price, the vendor will make his bid at or above the reserve price with the hope that someone else will bid a higher price than his vendor bid.

A property buyer has a lot working against him at an auction. On the flipside, observing other interested parties bidding allows the buyer to get a better understanding of the demand for a particular property. In essence, it's a double-edged sword. In a conventional non-auction-style sale, other interested parties are not in front of you and you are dependent on the real estate agent who is managing the negotiations of several parties—and that too makes the price rise just as easily.

Negative Gearing

On paper, Australians are awful property investors. Australian landlords lost $13.3 billion in 2011. Like most businesses, if you run your business at a loss, you will generally pay little or no income tax. In Australia, unless an investor in Australia lives in his own investment property, when an investor of any type in any industry borrows money to make an investment, the investor can reduce his tax burden by deducting the loss of operating the investment versus income. For example, Mr. Anderson is a plumber earning $70,000 per year, and he wants to purchase an investment property—a simple 2-bedroom apartment in a southern-Sydney neighborhood. The asking price for the investment property is $500,000. Mr. Anderson has a healthy savings account with a deposit of $100,000. His bank agrees to lend him $400,000 to purchase the property, plus another $17,990 to pay the stamp duty. With interest rates at record lows in Australia, he is offered a 25-year variable loan at 5% interest rate. Once purchased, a real estate agent then takes four weeks to find a tenant. Over that four-week period, Mr. Anderson is not making any revenue from this property investment, but he has bills such as debt, cleaning, maintenance and strata levies to pay. Mr. Anderson's mortgage repayment equates to roughly $708 per week, or $36,816 annually. In the initial phase of the loan, $401 of this is interest. During the first four tenantless weeks, Mr. Anderson may deduct this $401 interest payment from his $1346 weekly income. This leaves him with a weekly taxable income of $945 per week.

After four weeks, a tenant moves into Mr. Anderson's investment property, and he receives $360 per week rent. Because there is a $41-per-week difference in revenue versus interest repayment, Mr. Anderson is now able to deduct $41 per week from his taxable income versus the $401 a week he could deduct when the apartment was unoccupied.

Essentially, over a twelve-month period during which his apartment is occupied, he will spend $36,816 in mortgage repayments and receive rental revenues of $18,720. Because Mr. Anderson paid $20,852 just in interest, he will reduce his taxable income from $70,000 to $67,868. Like the majority of landlords who have purchased dwellings in the last four years, Mr. Anderson is not profiting from his investment. $100,000 deposit plus $36,816 in the first year alone is a big price to pay for any individual investor compared to the $18,720 in revenue. But now, instead of $400,000, he only owes the bank $384,000. That is nothing to write home about.

Australia must be the only place in the world where property investors think it's OK to run an investment property at a loss. If you're a landlord and have acquired a large debt to purchase an investment property, you're most probably spending more to hold your property than the amount you are receiving in rental revenue. For such a high price you don't get back much.

If you're buying an Australian home that you want to live in, you cannot negatively gear (claim tax deductions) on your property. But if you're a property investor seeking capital gain, that is not the right strategy. This is where things get tricky. Property investors who are seeking capital gain cannot exactly take advantage of negative gearing, as they want to live in their house for more than one year to avoid capital gain charges when they sell their property.

But Mr. Anderson will not be able to avoid capital gains tax, as he is not living in his investment property. If he holds his property for more than one year, he will be able to claim just a 50% reduction in CGT. In Australia, negative gearing is seen as a handy tool to help landlords reduce their tax burdens. In the rest of the world, negative gearing is seen as a tool to help those who have made a bad investment.

If, two years later, Mr. Anderson sells his property, he will have to sell the property for a much higher price than he purchased it for if he wants a net gain. This is because over the last two years he has paid a fraction more than $40,000 in interest and has only paid down $32,000 in principal from his mortgage. If Mr. Anderson is successful and sells his property for $575,000, is he able to make his money back in capital gain? Let's take a look:

Revenue	
Rent	$37,440
Costs	
Interest	$40,000
Stamp Duty	$17,990
Council rates	$2,300
Strata	$1,900
Real Estate Agent (2% of $600k)	$12,000
Maintenance and repairs	$3,200

Bank charges	$980
Utilities	$300
Legal	$1,300

Total= $79,970 — $37,440= $42,530

Total cost of property (not including any additional costs) is $542,530.

In a world that offers a wide variety of property investments, Mr. Anderson would have probably been better off making a property investment elsewhere. Depending on the additional costs on top of the above mentioned over the period of ownership, it is clear there was not much return for Mr. Anderson related to the overall risk he took. In Houston, the average gross rental yield of a property is close to 13%. By the time all bills and interest are paid, you are still a positively geared (versus negatively geared) Sydney investor, and you will probably end up with somewhere between 7% to 8% absolute annual return on investment with a fraction of the risk. This is what is worrying about Australia. In Houston, to attract the same rental revenue, a landlord needs to purchase a property within the $150,000 to $170,000 range. With significantly cheaper cost of living as compared to any major Australian city, Houstonians are able to purchase property with relatively small mortgages. Houstonians have a household median income almost equal to the median Australian household income. There is no need to negative gear when a landlord purchases a property in Houston or in the multitude of other U.S. cities that offer excellent yields for landlords. But then again, who can blame Mr. Anderson. He's a Sydneysider who is in the mindset to do what everyone else in Sydney and

Australia is trying to do—get into the property game. Australians are getting into the property game at a much higher price, and they have less room to navigate through any tough waters that may arise in the Australian property market. If you are a landlord in Houston and times get very tough, in the worst-case scenario, you will probably still be positively geared—A.K.A.: making money.

Debt and Property

Many residents of Ireland, Spain and the United States learned a valuable lesson in 2008. Too much debt can be dangerous. What was scary is that these three nations—"different" in culture, attitude and property-price-to-income ratios—all saw their property markets collapse. Why? Because the national mindsets in relation to real estate prices in their country changed on the back of limited access to debt. The American, Irish and Spanish property markets peaked at lower multiples than Australia's property market did, because, although compared to the value of their properties, banks were lending with a lower percentage deposit; they weren't lending the mass volume of debt relative to household income. For example, a family in Illinois buys a property for 4x the household income with 0% deposit. If that house is worth $200,000 and the annual household income is $50,000, the family should have greater ability to pay their debts than a median household in Sydney or Melbourne that requires 80% financing to buy their $900,000 dream home with $720,000 of debt to repay. Any pundit of the Australian real estate market must be able to make simple sense of what I am saying here. A debt of $720,000 for a household earning an annual income of $80,000 in Melbourne is more risky to the capital markets than an Illinois household buying a $200,000 home with no deposit but with $50,000 annual income. In the absolute worst-case scenario, the lender in Illinois will lose $200,000—but the lender in Melbourne can lose up to $720,000. This difference is enormous.

The worst part of the real estate game is the collateral that needs to be initially put down in order to access financing in Australia. Yes, a homebuyer in Australia generally requires a 20% deposit or collateral to get a loan from one of the Big 4. But how are first homeowners coming up with large deposits to purchase a home in an over-priced property market? There are a number of ways. Of course there are cash-savvy individuals who spend several years saving up enough money to make a 20% deposit on a new home. But, more likely, first-time Australian buyers—in particular those looking in the more expensive property markets—are getting a lot of help from their parents. Parents of new homeowners are probably contributing more than they should, putting their children, and themselves, in the firing line of banks if something should go wrong. There are too many parents using their homes, or other equity, as guarantee to the banks should their children fail to meet the financial obligations of a loan. But this is the reality of the Australian property market today.

If you aren't Australian, let me tell you—Australia is definitely "different" than the rest of the world. It is very expensive to live in Australia. I've just returned to the southern beaches of Sydney after nine years of living in the expensive locales of Switzerland and

Central London, and I feel like my bank account empties faster here than when I lived in Europe. It truly feels like I'm paying Swiss prices for the cost of living. But when I look at the newspaper's real estate section, Australia looks much more pricey than Switzerland; and the average Swiss income is higher than the average Australian income.

It doesn't matter what a pundit says, the facts are on the balance sheets of the financial institutions. A quick look at the balance sheet of any of the Big 4 banks, or the private sector debt data taken from the Australian bureau of statistics or the Trading Economics website reveals that Australian households have enormous exposure to debt.

I would agree that responsible lending helps to create long-term sustainable growth. But when capital growth is dependent on interest rates and the willingness of banks' to lend excessively, problems inevitably arise. If the banks stopped lending to property buyers tomorrow, do you think that there would be just as much demand for property in the Australian housing market on the part of Australian citizens and residents? Of course not! It's no surprise that Demographia's annual housing-affordability survey reveals that none of the housing markets in Australia's major cities are classified as affordable or moderately affordable. Sydney, Melbourne, Brisbane, Perth and Adelaide are all classified as having "severely unaffordable" property markets. According to Demographia, a seriously unaffordable property market is one where median property values are between 4.1x to 5x the incomes. Severely unaffordable is classified as being 5.1x the household income or higher. Of the thirty-nine property markets in Australia examined by Demographia, twenty-five were classified as severely unaffordable and the remaining fourteen markets were classified as seriously unaffordable. There are more severely and seriously unaffordable property markets in Australia than there are in all of the United States.

For all of the thirty-nine largest property markets in Australia to have a property-price-to-household-income ratio of 4.1 or higher clearly indicates that, across the country, banks and mortgage lenders are recklessly lending to property buyers. With household debt in Australia now averaging around $180,000 per household, there is very little room to navigate through an economic shock to the system. The property market has not truly been tested to see if it could weather tough financial headwinds.

Interest-only debt

To make matters worse, the hypothetical Mr. Anderson who took on $400,000 in debt and seeks to pay off all the principal of the mortgage over a 25-year period looks responsible when compared to the majority of current Australian property purchasers. Yes, banks have become more risky in their lending practices than ever before. Why? Interest-only debt. Interest-only debt for homebuyers is a loan where the borrower doesn't make principal payments to drive down the overall debt burden over a period of time. For example, Mr. Smith purchases the $500,000 apartment next to Mr. Anderson. Like Mr. Anderson, Mr. Smith uses $100,000 from his savings for the 20% deposit. The bank offers Mr. Smith a $400,000 interest-only loan. Unlike Mr. Anderson, who is paying on average $708 per week in interest and principal to the bank, Mr. Smith is only paying back $401 in interest to the bank—he is not paying down the principal. Mr. Smith believes that the value of the property will double in five years. His strategy is to live in the property for five years, and then sell it at double the purchase price.

If Mr. Smith sells the apartment for $1 million in five years, and interest rates don't change, he will only pay roughly $80,000 in interest over that five-year period. By the time all costs are calculated, Mr. Smith will probably end up with somewhere between $250,000 to $300,000 in tax-free capital gain. On the flipside, if a shock to the Australian housing market starts to bring prices down after Mr. Smith has made the purchase, he will be in a lot of trouble. Why? If the value of the apartment falls below the purchase price, he will be holding an underwater mortgage. If five years after Mr. Smith purchased the $500,000 property, he sells it for $350,000, he will still owe the bank $400,000. Mr. Smith will have to pay the difference of $50,000 out of his own pocket. When you factor in the $80,000 in interest paid over the five years, Mr. Smith has a total loss of $230,000. That's without adding all the other costs involved, such as stamp duty, real estate agent fees, and all the other costs he cannot claim back against his income because he was living in his own dwelling to take advantage of the CGT. In short, this is an investment gone very bad.

With a growing amount of Australian property buyers taking on interest-only debt, the ramifications of a declining property market are severe.

Property prices in Australia were not always disproportionate to incomes

Historically, it has only been over the last fifteen years that housing prices have leaped higher versus household incomes versus the historic trend. Between 1991 and 2000, Sydney's property-price-to-income ratio climbed from around 5x to 6x. Melbourne spiked from 4x to 6x. Between 2001 and 2013, the ratios in Sydney and Melbourne have jumped to 9x and 8.4x, respectively. Relative to incomes, it is clear that Sydneysiders are paying close to double what they were twenty years ago for a property. Melbournians are paying more than double. Perth and Brisbane residents are also paying double relative to incomes. In Adelaide, they are close to paying double as well. Over the last 15 years, the property-price-to-income ratio on average has increased annually in Sydney and Melbourne by approximately 0.26x annual household income. Adelaide, Brisbane and Perth's markets have increased by around 0.20x annual income.

If property prices return to long-term historic price levels relative to household income, the collateral damage to the Australian economy and homeowners will be extensive. For example, Sydney's January 2014 median house price was $763,000. Factoring in wage increases over the last several months, household income in Sydney is roughly $76,400. This leaves us with a property-price-to-income ratio of 9.89. If property prices in Sydney return to the historic 5x income range to purchase property, the average price of a Sydney property will drop to roughly $382,000. This is a price drop of almost 50%. If the other major cities in Australia return to historic trends, one cannot describe the impact it will make on the greater Australian economy. Sydney, for example, hasn't had a median house price of $382,000 since 2001. Hundreds of billions would be wiped off the balance sheets of households and banks. But the amount of debt owed to creditors would remain the same. This is generally what happens when a bubble pops.

Because of the sheer sum value of Australian real estate in addition to inflated house-price-to-income ratios, any small drop in housing prices can have a significant impact on the economy. But for households in major Australian cities, it takes between a 9% (Sydney) to 18% (Brisbane) drop in property prices for households to lose the equivalent of a year's income on the asset value of their properties.

Over the last twenty-five years, there have only been a slight handful of occasions where a little air was taken out of the Australian property bubble. This concerns me—the larger the rise, the harder the fall. The Australian housing bubble has essentially been pumped up with debt. And each year the banks have to lend more to homebuyers than they did the previous year in order to increase their profit margin. Most Australian homebuyers who have purchased a property with a 20% deposit or less in the last five to six years will most probably have an underwater mortgage within the next three years if one of several possible economic triggers sends shockwaves through the Australian economy.

Chapter Eight

Politicians and Reserve Bankers:

Where did they go wrong?

Politicians and central bankers around the world are constantly being challenged by various economic encounters. Managing economic growth and inflation, and reducing unemployment, are the main objectives of a central bank. When inflation rises within a country, the central bank will increase interest rates to slow it down. When unemployment rises, central bankers bring interest rates down to stimulate employment. When economic growth excels beyond a reasonable speed, they move interest rates higher. Interest rates are lowered when the adverse occurs.

When a sharp economic shock hits an economy, the central bank will generally take more measures beyond their normal function to help alleviate pain in a damaged economy. In the United States, the Federal Reserve launched a quantitative easing (QE) program on the back of the incredible economic downturn during the GFC. This was an unconventional approach by the central bank. The strategy to purchase securities in the marketplace, such as bonds and distressed mortgages, was implemented to better dictate the over-all movement of money. The objective was to alleviate the American private-sector debt burden and stop the U.S. government from paying higher interest rates on the bonds they issue while stimulating the domestic economy. The result: economic pain was artificially sucked out of the system, and the central bank absorbed the unconventional monetary policy on its balance sheet. Over the course of QE in the United States, the Dow Jones and S&P 500 have both more than doubled in value. "Don't fight with the Fed" was the common advice given by institutional investors. Why? Because when the U.S. Federal Reserve pumps hundreds of billions into the system, it inflates it with the hope that one day the economy will no longer require the stimulus and the central bank can taper off its involvement and let the economy run on its own accord.

After several years of QE in the United States, the time has now come for the Federal Reserve to taper its asset-purchase program. New Federal Reserve Chairman, Janet Yellen, is following the strategy of her predecessor, Ben Bernanke, to taper QE in order to let the economy run on its own two feet.

In Japan at the end of 2012, Prime Minister Shinzo Abe launched a stimulus program now known as "Abenomics." The strategy to stimulate the economy by pumping tens of trillions of yen into the system would have its targeted short-term effects and objectives met. This is not the first time the Japanese have attempted to artificially stimulate the economy. But still, Japan's economy has achieved very little growth over the last two decades, with growth being volatile, and Japan's economy falling in and out of recession. GDP in Japan either slowly creeps up for a short period of time or it dwindles down. Japan's economy nosedived more than two decades ago when its credit bubble collapsed and sent inflated property prices crashing to below-historic levels. Of any major economy, Japan has felt the worst effects of easy lending and allowing the system to absorb a significant amount of debt without managing it. During the late 1980s, the Japanese central bank and politicians made a horrendous error of judgment. This led to Japan going through a "lost decade." Homeowners, banks and companies took on leverage at an alarming rate. Because the economy was growing, politicians and central bankers in Japan didn't want to interrupt strong growth. The balance sheet of the private sector in Japan was overloaded with assets, with little cash to cover any potential shock to the economy. By the early 90s, house by house, bank by bank, business by business, Japanese would not be able to cover their debts. One after another, businesses were dropping like flies and homeowners were going underwater with their debts.

When politicians and central banks fall asleep at the wheel, the result is generally catastrophic. Just like those in Japan, the U.S. central bankers and politicians fell asleep at the wheel in the first half of the 2000s. You never heard the word bubble. Excess credit in the market fueled rising home prices, and central bankers and politicians justified the rise of the stock market. Essentially, in regards to economics, history has a good track record of repeating itself. Central bankers and politicians who do not identify that there is a credit or property bubble (or both) in their economy will find themselves proven wrong. Historically, the laws of economics usually wins. You don't have to have a PhD in economics to assess whether there is a credit or property bubble within a domestic economy. But the bubbles tend to get overshadowed by pundits. Politicians and central bankers will stand by banking and real estate pundits in order to back the strong growth of their economy. This is precisely what has happened in Australia, and history will repeat itself.

After recent years of Labor Party (ALP) rule, Australia had a change of government in 2013. The Liberal Party (LIB) returned to power with Tony Abbott as the Prime Minister and Joe Hockey as the Treasurer. The ALP experienced economic growth throughout the course of its tenure governing Australia. In my opinion there is no other political party in history that had so much luck. The ALP came to power in 2007 under the leadership of Kevin Rudd. Julia Gilard took over as prime minister in 2010, and Wayne Swan was the Treasurer for both Prime Ministers until Rudd won back leadership of the ALP in 2013, just prior to the party's election defeat.

The Reserve Bank of Australia (RBA) is the nation's central bank. It supposedly acts independently. Although this is arguable, the RBA plays a significant role in relation to the Australian economy. Like many central banks throughout the world, the RBA dictates the interest rate, and manages inflation and the local currency. The RBA gives the public valuable insight into the state of the Australian economy and where it is heading. The RBA makes regular economic forecasts that are used by the greater public to make investment decisions. Since 2006, the RBA has been led by Governor Glenn Stevens.

In 2006, the Australian economy was a USD$692 billion economy. By 2013, it was a USD$1.520-trillion economy. The reason I mention Australia's GDP in $USD is because it reflects several dynamics. The Australian currency was around parity in 2013 versus hovering between the $0.70c to $0.80c range just eight years prior. In 2011, the $AUD peaked at $1.10c, and by mid 2013, it was sitting at around $1.05c. Since then, the $AUD has fallen below parity against the USD, and is now hovering around the $0.90c mark. The recent fall in the Australian currency can be contributed to two key factors. The first factor is that the RBA reduced interest rates over the previous twenty-five months, and more important, there was a big short on the $AUD by hedge fund owner George Soros, which sent the $AUD below parity. Mr. Soros has quite the impressive track record in currency trading.

In 2006, interest rates in Australia were hovering around the 5.5% range, and they peaked in 2008 at 7.25%. By that time, reality had set in regarding the global economic problems. The RBA had reduced interest rates down to 3% by 2009. Over the coming years, the reserve rate climbed up to 4.75%, and as of 2014, the rate is at an historic low of 2.5%. It's definitely an unusual central bank policy to have record-low interest rates at a point in time when private sector debt continues to grow at a stifling pace. Furthermore, property remains out of reach for first-time homebuyers, and more important, there is no recession. Unemployment is still relatively low, and the miners are exporting more iron ore than ever. So why on earth are interest rates at a historically low level? Because the RBA believes that the currency is too high on the back of the second pillar peaking its intensive capital expenditure cycle. From now on, annual capital expenditure on new mine developments will start to decrease year after year. The RBA wants the real estate sector and rest of the Australian economy to pick up the slack.

The RBA and the federal government want the Australian economy to adapt to changing times. With the mining sector now more focused on extracting iron ore rather than building new mine sites, it's inevitable that jobs will be lost within the sector. Furthermore, fixed investments into the mining sector will continue to decline. So the RBA has reduced interest rates to stimulate the non-mining sectors of the Australian economy. Great! Now that interest rates are at an all-time low, the first pillar of the Australian economy has been lending at a toxic level to Pillar Three. Not so great! Housing prices have increased across the nation. The credit bubble is getting bigger, and it has all been invested into one sector of the Australian economy. Does the RBA think there is a property bubble in Australia? No! In fact, the RBA is reducing interest rates to stimulate the construction of housing and the price of property—because who is going to buy a dwelling, knock it down, and build a new dwelling in the midst of falling house prices? It is clear that even with record-low interest rates, there's no evidence to suggest that the parts of the Australian economy that lie outside the pillars are big enough to fill the future shortfall from the reduction in capital expenditure from the mining sector. All bets are now on housing.

I think it's pretty clear that the RBA pulled the trigger way too soon. **Australia is not in recession right now**. The RBA has made an enormous error of judgment. And as of 2014, the Australian housing bubble is being inflated on top of its already-inflated pricing levels. The worst thing about a credit-backed housing bubble is that it puts enormous pressure on homebuyers if there is any shock to the market, while forecasting long-term Chinese economic growth. I truly fear that Australia has too much air in the bubble to be able to dodge any more shocks to the economy. Why? Because when you have private sector debt that is 20% greater than GDP, there is absolutely zero room for error. The mere fact that the bulk of this private sector debt is tied up in housing makes it impossible to imagine that the Australian property-price-to-income ratio can be minimized through increased wages. The ratio difference will only come down by households defaulting on their mortgages.

I believe the RBA will inevitably have to increase interest rates. By pulling the trigger too early, the RBA has allowed the Australian credit bubble to get bigger. And in a desperate hour when Australian households need the RBA to cut interest rates the most, they will find the RBA will have to raise interest rates—because the $AUD is on its way down. The cost of foreign goods is increasing faster than anticipated. More importantly, sooner rather than later, China is going to wake up and realize that it has built the largest property bubble in human history. The Chinese bubble is fueled by an unimaginable amount of off-balance-sheet debt. If there is a credit crunch in China, a lot of this debt is essentially outside the scope of being bailed out. If the mining sector contributed to the rise of the $AUD, it will most certainly contribute to the fall of the $AUD. The RBA has brought interest rates down too low to specifically reduce the value of the $AUD. Interest rates and a strong $AUD were the two influential buffers that were keeping a level of pressure on the three pillars. Such pressure that was stopping them from getting more out of control than they already were. Reducing interest rates without a recession at this point in time in the Australian economy has inevitably put Australia's economy on the chopping block.

The Bubble should have popped in 2008

If Australia's credit bubble had popped back in 2008, the Australian economy would be in a much better situation in 2014. As bad as they are, recessions can improve an economy's business model over the long term. Like a housekeeper, a recession arrives, cleans up the mess, and then leaves. The longer you wait to clean your place, the longer it takes the housekeeper to clean up the mess. And it hits the wallet harder when you have to make one big payment to a housekeeper. Following a 2008 recession, households and banks would have had less debt on their balance sheets. The mining sector would have provided a buffer to alleviate Australia from being in recession for too long. It was the ultimate and only chance the Australian economy had to clear up its mess. More importantly, Australians would have been better educated about the risks involved when taking on too much debt to buy property.

But since that moment in 2008, the bubble has only gotten bigger and bigger. It has essentially become irreparable. Based on the economic forecasts, there is no possible way that incomes can ever catch up with property prices. Property prices can only come down to bring common sense to the existing ratios that suggest Australia's property market is in a long-term chronic bubble cycle. The lack of cyclic activity in the Australian economy also distorts the inevitable downturn. After a quarter century of growth, it's going to take the housekeeper a lot longer to clean up the mess when a trigger sends the Australian economy into a nosedive. It's only then that we will truly see how reckless banks were with their lending habits.

Reducing interest rates too early will inevitably backfire and affect more Australians than were affected in the 1991 recession. This leads to the issue of leadership. Why did the RBA and the Rudd government stimulate the economy in 2008? One thing is for sure, the Australian economy would have gone into recession or depression if China hadn't gone on an infrastructure spending spree. In 2008/2009 the Rudd government stimulated the Australian economy by pumping $48 billion into the system through giving close to $1,000 to every Australian earning under $80,000, alongside a host of other perks. It is my opinion that the Rudd and Gillard governments and the RBA have been managing the Australian credit bubble, rather than managing the Australian economy. This is the priority of Australian leadership, and it has distorted their views on what defines excessive lending. They don't want the credit bubble to pop. Wayne Swan was probably the weakest Treasurer in modern Australian history. Mr. Swan just let everything grow out of control, and Australians will pay for his economic mismanagement probably sometime over the next three years—because sometimes it takes that long for reality to kick in. In 2012, Asian-economics commentator Andy Xie stated that Australia would face similar challenges to those that Spain faced during the GFC. At that point in time, the biggest pundit of the Australian economy, Mr. Swan, responded on CNBC:

"It's absurd—the Australian economy and its economic fundamentals are very strong. On a yearly basis we are growing at 4%—we are going to grow faster than any other developed economy this year and next. Let's go through the fundamentals—bringing our budget back to surplus in 2012-2013, low unemployment, strong job creation over time, a record investment pipeline in resources—half a trillion (dollars). What planet does he live on?"

I'm not sure how the former Treasurer feels today about making this comment, but what we do know is that Andy Xie is from planet Earth, and he simply had a valid view. But the pundit got the last word. Now look at the Australian economy today versus Mr. Swan's predictions. It's worth breaking down his comments to see where the Australian economy actually is.

> "The Australian economy and its economic fundamentals are very strong."

The fundamentals of the Australian economy are not strong. The domestic economy is fueled by excessive debt.

> "On a yearly basis we are growing at 4%— we are going to grow faster than any other developed economy this year and next"

Not the case.

"Low unemployment, strong job creation over time, a record investment pipeline in resources—half a trillion (dollars)."

Unemployment is rising at a fairly fast pace, and that investment pipeline ended up being smaller than half a trillion dollars because there have been close to $100 billion in cancelled investments since Treasurer Swan made this statement. When Mr. Hockey was interviewed on CNBC in 2013, he made a defensive case that the Australian property market was not in a bubble. Although he makes similar commentary in the international public arena, domestically, current Treasurer, Joe Hockey, is sending Australians a much different message. He is using tough gestures to suggest Australia's future is in for troubled times. Hockey regularly emphasizes that wages in Australia are very high, which challenges Australia's competitiveness, and that there's a budget crisis that will take years to get the government budget back into surplus. He is not afraid to admit that jobs will be lost throughout the course of 2014, and he's not willing to bail out the troubled industries outside the three pillars. From the subtle but stern messages sent across the newswires, it seems as though the Abbott-led government understands there is trouble brewing for the Australian economy—because, overall, the economy is not growing at anywhere near the same pace that it has been over the last few years. But once again, today's value of real estate is defended by the new Prime Minister, his Treasurer, and the bulk of politicians in the federal and state governments of Australia.

Just think about it. Australian government debt is on the increase at a fast rate. Since the GFC, the Australian government has run a deficit year after year. Government debt totaled just $58 billion in 2007, and it jumped to $247 billion by 2013. Imagine if the property bubble had popped back in 2008 and property prices had returned to the relative norm versus household incomes. There would be a very good chance that property investors/landlords would not be running their investments at a loss. There would be no need for negative gearing because residential rental rates generally don't fall as hard as property prices do. The $20 billion in annual write-downs and negative gearing-related activities linked to property investment would not occur. If property was positively geared, it would in one way or another bring close to $7 billion a year in extra government revenue. Instantaneously, government deficits in Australia would have been roughly 22% smaller over the last six years. In a nutshell, property investors as a whole would be at least $120 billion better off. Over the last six years, Australian government debt would be at least $42 billion less. In 2008, political and central bank leaders in Australia unfortunately could not see the big opportunity that was missed. Leaders were focused on solving a short-term problem. Their solution has caused inevitable long-term problems for Australia.

How much longer can Australia's leaders turn a blind eye to the credit-fueled property bubble?

Australia's political and financial leaders have turned a blind eye to the dangers of sky-high property prices for far too long. But my question to the leaders is this: At what household leverage ratio will you have to slam on the brakes to bring down property prices? When will you introduce measures to reduce the overall risk that a homebuyer can take in order to purchase a dwelling? At the current rate of growth, as the last half of 2013 suggests, Sydney will soon have a household leverage ratio of 10x. This is crazy. Sydney is the largest city in Australia, and its residents are already highly overleveraged. If the Sydney property market goes down, it will take the rest of Australia down with it. Once again, the leaders of Australia should have popped the bubble back in 2008. If they had, banks would have been forced to diversify their investment portfolios.

Australia has a lot of expertise in three industries: Natural Resources, Housing, and Banking. With the pillars inhaling the bulk of private investment, little credit is left for the hundreds of other industries across Australia. The carbon tax in Australia is a controversial tax. The one thing the ALP did make a concerted effort to tackle was the reduction of Australia's carbon emissions through taxing those who are the biggest polluters. To my understanding, the idea was to make companies invest locally in finding technical solutions that would reduce the amount of carbon tax they would owe by reducing the amount of carbon emitted into the air. Unfortunately, Australia is not an innovative country. Yes, Australia has great engineers busy in the second pillar of the Australian economy. But apart from that, Australia falls behind on the innovation curve, because Australian businesses do not invest as much as they should in innovation. Once again, a missed opportunity to build a new Australian economy. If Australian businesses invested as much in technical innovation to solve their carbon tax bills as they did lobbying for reducing carbon tax, Australia may have had a new industry by now.

Leadership has not kept up with changing times

Today I work in the clean technology sector, and I see how Australia is well behind the innovation curve versus other Western nations. It is deeply saddening. And I am a true believer that government should not be involved in investing in innovation. It is the private sector that should invest in and reap the rewards of innovation. But in Australia, leadership does not do enough to convince the private sector to invest in innovation. The Gillard government tried to invest billions in innovation. But when government backs innovation, it becomes incredibly expensive versus the potential return on investment. Private sector-funded innovation is forced to come up with cost-effective solutions. This is the difference. Commercial viability. Therefore, the mindset is not there for Australian businesses to invest in the development of new technologies. The best Australian engineers outside of the mining industry are overseas or probably working for an overseas multinational, securing their futures. Aside from the three pillars, Australia doesn't have much to offer the world apart from agriculture. Silicon Valley is the home of innovation. It rewards innovation and some of the world's most innovative companies are based there. Innovators and entrepreneurs from around the world make their pilgrimages to this valley of talent. **And in Silicon Valley it's ok to fail. In Australia it's not ok to fail. The mindset is simply not there**. Unless Australian leadership rewards risk outside of the three pillars, Australia will only head backwards.

If you're a politician in Australia, you're committing political suicide if you talk down property; that's how passionate Australians are about real estate—they will throw you out of office very quickly if you talk down property. If the Abbott government makes no concerted effort to improve housing affordability, the market will inevitably do it for him. It is always better to intentionally let a bit of air out of the credit bubble than to let it burst in one big pop. Unfortunately, Australia is probably past a point where there exists a feasible strategy to reshape the Australian economy without significantly increasing the private sector debt levels. It must not be easy for a Prime Minister and a nation to realize that in order for Australia to grow, the economy needs to be broadly diversified; but when you have three pillars that have absorbed roughly 85% of available credit (equal to more than 100% of GDP), you cannot change the strategy without inflicting pain.

Unfortunately for Julia Gillard, Australia's first woman prime minister, she had all the opportunity in the world to take action. Under her tenure, private sector debt has skyrocketed, and businesses outside the three pillars are struggling—because in Australia there is the dangerous cocktail of high rent and high wages. The retail sector (which has struggled as the three pillars have grown) is forced to pay higher rents and higher wages. That's why shopping in Australia is so expensive. Under Ms. Gillard's watch, industries outside the three pillars have been hit with this double whammy of high costs, and the effect of this flows throughout the economy. It extracts more money out of the bank accounts of households. This is essentially where leadership has failed to manage the impact of having three thriving industries that went unmanaged. Prime Minister Gillard was asleep at the wheel. And Australia is now paying for it, and will suffer from it over the next few years.

The RBA has also been asleep at the wheel. The Australian economy has essentially passed a point of no return, and just the slightest trigger could send the Australian economy into a downward spiral. For job growth in Australia, businesses outside the three pillars need to reduce costs elsewhere. For the majority of businesses, rent is the only fixed cost that could be reduced enough to cover the cost of adding more human talent to improve shareholder value. This is how important the property market is to the RBA. The RBA would have popped the bubble by now if they were trying to avoid another moment of insanity in the history of economics. The Australian economy needs structural change. You cannot have both high wages and high cost of real estate. It simply kills business and stops energetic entrepreneurs from taking risks in industries outside the three pillars. Either wages need to go down or rent does. One way or another, the RBA needs to pop the property bubble or the government needs to reduce wages. Either choice will drive Australia into recession; but either choice is better than letting the market decide to take the Australian economy down.

Leadership in Australia needs to make the tough decisions. The Abbott government and the RBA should be more concerned with popping the property bubble than trying to nickel and dime its way into prosperity—this hurts the wrong subsectors of the Australian population. When a government tries to nickel and dime its way out of a tax revenue challenge, they hurt families, low-income earners, and those in need. They should be more focused on the industry that profits the most in capital gain but pays the least in taxes—the real estate industry.

The Abbott government has indeed inherited Australia at a time when it must be visible that the Gillard strategy is not working. Does the Abbott leadership have the willpower to pop the Australian bubble? Or will the leadership let the market decide to pop the bubble? The Japanese and the Americans know the wrath of a market-led recession. It's not a pretty sight. But for Australia, the clock is ticking. There is no doubt that China will reduce its demand for iron ore. Once reality sets into the Chinese real estate market, the emerging world will enter into an economic free fall. Australia is a Western economy that placed the biggest macroeconomic bet in its history on the idea that China will only grow. Unfortunately, nobody in government or the RBA seems to have calculated the floor space that is constructed annually in China, and nor have they figured out that China will build a dwelling for every man, woman and child in just a few years from now. I highly doubt China will go that far. Waking up to reality will inevitably stop growth in China. Unfortunately, Australia missed its golden opportunity to prick the credit bubble back in 2008. But if the government deliberately drives the Australian economy into recession, this act will provide just enough buffer to soften the blow ever so slightly—which is important. Why? Would you rather the Australian GDP drop by 4% or 9%+? That is the difference between the effect of a government-driven recession and a market-driven recession.

The last few paragraphs present a very rare negative assessment of the Australian economy. But the fact of the matter is that Australia is already experiencing a toxic credit bubble. Households have a chronic addiction to debt, and the banks supply the addiction. Taking the toxic fumes out of the toxic bubble with an orchestrated strategy will take the bite out of the potential losses experienced as external forces drive down the mining sector and cause a domino effect. When China stops constructing residential property, other large trading partners in the Asia-Pacific region will also be part of the collateral damage. Indonesia, Korea, Japan, Singapore and Malaysia will each take one very big hit. Like Australia, they are in no position to absorb the damaging effects of the greatest property bubble in human history. And like Australian politicians, leaders around the Asia-Pacific region apparently had no calculator on hand to do the proper mathematics. At the end of the day, history will once again show political and central bank leaders that it cannot be defied. Taking the side of the pundits with flawed data is never a good strategy.

Today's politicians from both sides of politics are not taking action like politicians did during the Hawke/Keating and Howard/Costello eras. It would be incredibly challenging for the Abbott/Hockey leadership to pass structural reform through the senate. One only has to look at the Australian economy in the 1980s and see the foundations that set Australia up for a recession. Although not anywhere near the same scale, Australia was in a similar situation back in the late '80s. The 1990-1991 recession is well documented in the Australian history books. Now might be a good time for politicians to understand what caused that recession—the challenge back then was only a fraction of today's challenge.

What frustrates me the most about Australia is that it feels like the country has been indoctrinated with the idea that the good times will never end, that property prices only rise, that the Chinese economy will never collapse, and that China will always purchase everything Australian miners extract from the ground. Australian leadership lacks expertise regarding how to prepare the nation for a shock to the economic system. It was not that long ago that the American economy faced its biggest financial storm in our lifetime, and Australian leadership learned absolutely nothing from it. Is Australia really different, or is it just naïve? My answer to this question is that Australian leaders are not naïve—they just got cocky. The leaders had no clue regarding the long-term effects of the clear lack of strategy that has lasted over the last six years. Just sitting back and enjoying the good times is not a strategy in the midst of a mining boom. This is the biggest mistake Australian leadership has ever made. We learned nothing from the mistakes of others, and that is why Australian leadership will be forever viewed as naïve. Worst of all, at a government, corporate and household level, Australia lacks expertise to manage recession. We only know how to manage bubbles. This is where the RBA and the Australian government went wrong.

Chapter Nine

Scenario One:

The International Event that Causes a Domino Effect

Nobody has a crystal ball that can tell the future. However, to better improve the chances of making an accurate forecast, data is analyzed, we know history repeats itself and there are algorithms that can be developed to better help identify possible scenarios that can cause an economic downturn. When an economy is growing but looking like it has froth, very rarely does anyone predict to the week when a downturn begins. And sometimes, economic forecasts just simply never come to fruition.

Over the next two chapters I will provide commentary on two possible scenarios. Although these scenarios have real possibilities of coming to fruition, I am presenting them as being hypothetical. I do not have a crystal ball, but based on my research, these are two possible scenarios that I believe Australia will witness sometime over the next one to three years. And for the sake of simplicity, I will use dollars instead of yuan in these scenarios.

Scenario One

It's a typical smoggy, humid dawn in June 2015 in southern China. A fourth-tier city that we will call 4A lies 250 km north of the first-tier city of Guangzhou. Across the horizon from 4A cranes crowd the skyline. At ground level there is hardly a car in sight in the central district of this city. In June of 2014, there were 350,000 apartments under construction within the city limits of 4A. City 4A has a population of 300,000 people, and the local government forecast that the population would grow by 1.4 million in the next seven years alone. On the top floor of a new apartment building is a 27-year-old construction worker named Mr. Hong. He hammers the last nail of the construction site into the wall, and his fellow construction workers cheer. Mr. Hong and his colleagues are very proud of finishing their fifteenth building site in just four years. He has been working on this particular site for four months, and the next day he and his colleagues will begin to build a new apartment complex a mile down the road. Mr. Hong earns roughly $4,000 a year as a construction worker, and he is a very responsible saver. By managing to live life in a very cost-efficient manner, he has been saving $1,200 a year for the last eight years of work.

Like many Chinese, Mr. Hong wants to own property. In order to boost his savings, he opted to invest in a structured investment product sold through his retail bank (Bank A). Bank A doesn't own this product, but sells it exclusively on behalf of the investment company (shadow bank) that will take Mr. Hong's money and offer a 10% annual return. Why does Mr. Hong want his money to go into a shadow banking fund? Because the retail banks don't offer the generous interest rates that the shadow banks do. Bank A only offers Mr. Hong an interest rate of 3% if he holds his money in his account. In China, 3% interest doesn't cover the shortfall once inflation is factored in. So, at the age of 19, Mr. Hong told Bank A that he wanted to invest in a financial product managed by a shadow bank to seek better yields on the cash he would save up over his career. In 2006, Bank A advised Mr. Hong to invest in a fund called the "China Fast Growth Fund" (CFGF). Mr. Hong invested his money in this fund because it gave him an annual interest rate of 10% versus 3% at the retail banks. In June 2011, the CFGF fund matured, and the $3,000 he invested was returned to him on top of the $1,500 in interest he received over the five-year period. Mr. Hong was very happy with the investment he had made and put the $4,500 in savings along with the $1,000 he saved in the last twelve months ($5,500 in total) into the new CFGC fund that is due to mature in June 2015. Bank A would always remind Mr. Hong that the CFGF fund was safe and he could pull his money out whenever he wanted, which brought that extra little peace of mind. And each year, Mr. Hong put $1,000 into the fund as he saved through the course of his career. Fast-forward to June 2015 and Mr. Hong is now at a point where he can really consider purchasing a property. Property prices keep skyrocketing in China year after year, so he is eager to get in the game.

The apartments in the new construction site where Mr. Hong is working have a starting price of $75,000 with 100% upfront payment for a 60m2 2-bedroom apartment. This is $8,000 off the selling price, because Mr. Hong is working at the site and he would pay 100% upfront for the property before it has even been built. Even with Mr. Hong now having close to $10,000 in savings, the price for an apartment in this complex is slightly out of his price range. But instead of just telling himself that it's out of his price range, he thinks about it some more. He walks into the sales office and sees what the apartment complex will look like when his team finishes building it in four months. The salesman of the complex pitches the benefits gained from investing in the building, saying that the complex will be lively, fresh and modern. He also thinks it will be fun to live alongside the wealthier residents of the town. Buy today for $75,000, he says, and next year it will be worth $90,000—because property prices only go up in City 4A. Ten years from now every apartment in 4A will be occupied with homeowners and renters. "You can't lose!"

The salesman introduces Mr. Hong to his associate who specializes in arranging financing solutions for individuals like Mr. Hong. The finance specialist tells Mr. Hong that he can arrange financing for him through a preferred shadow bank at the rate of 12% per year. The shadow bank that will give him the loan is called the Incredible Homes Mortgage Fund (IMF). The specialist reminds Mr. Hong that it would be near impossible for him to get a $65,000 mortgage from the retail bank with just a $10,000 deposit. But the finance specialist is concerned that he will be able to pay the 12% interest and principal of $10,000 per year, which is higher than his annual income of $4,000 (which next month rises to $5,000 a year). Mr. Hong does some calculations to see how big of a deposit he needs to bring the annual interest and principal repayments down to $3,000. Because he has close to $10,000 saved in cash, he needs to borrow $65,000—but even his soon-to-be $5,000 a year income will not be enough to cover the payments. Mr. Hong calculates his cost of living and the impact it will make on his income. Mr. Hong already pays $100 a month in rent, so he will be able to use that $1,200 to pay off a mortgage rather than pay rent. On top of that, he will be saving $1,000 a year, so he'll have $3,200 a year to pay in interest and principal. Mr. Hong says that he will be visiting his parents soon. When he comes back, he hopes to have a bigger deposit so he will be able to pay less in interest.

That weekend, Mr. Hong visits his parents, who have saved close to $90,000 for their retirement. Mr. Hong's parents agree that he needs some help to secure his future, and they value the importance of having a roof over his head because owning a home will make life easier for Mr. Hong. In China, if you don't own a home, it is more difficult to get a date. In China, it's no secret that one of the most important qualities a Chinese woman looks for in a man is homeownership. If a man doesn't own a home, he is seen as shameful and poor. The parents discuss between themselves and offer to give their son a helping hand. They will give Mr. Hong $40,000 of their savings to help purchase his first home. Mr. Hong is happy as can be. His parents know that this loan will make their retirement years much tougher, but they love their son and want to see him happy.

Two days later, Mr. Hong is back at the construction site. At lunchtime he walks into the sales office and tells the salesman that he would like to purchase a bottom-of-the-range apartment for $75,000. With a $50,000 deposit, Mr. Hong only needs a $25,000 loan. The finance specialist in the sales office sits with Mr. Hong and says, " Mr. Hong, you don't need such a big deposit! Just pay a $40,000 deposit and then use the $10,000 you have saved in the CFGF fund that matures later this month to pay down some principal and reinvest the rest to help you build a long-term safety net." Mr. Hong appreciates the advice and takes it. But in the eyes of the finance specialist, he has gotten IMF a safe customer compared to the 85% leverage ratio the bulk of the other mortgage holders have taken on. Even though Mr. Hong will pay 12% interest and principal to IMF on $35,000 instead of $25,000, he thinks it's a good deal. He now has 100% up front to pay for the apartment. The salesman and the finance specialist print out the paperwork for Mr. Hong and he signs on the dotted line. They all shake hands and Mr. Hong goes back to the building he will soon live in and works harder than ever to make sure this building is the best he has ever built. "Only four months to go," he thinks. While Mr. Hong is back at work, the finance specialist arranges with the property salesman the transfer of funds from the IMF to the property developer. The property developer has made a great deal from Mr. Hong's paying upfront.

As the end of June 2015 nears, Mr. Hong receives his paycheck and sends his first mortgage payment to IMF. The first eight months of this mortgage is going to be hell for Mr. Hong because he has to pay back $550 monthly in interest and principal. But with $1,500 in his bank account, $10,000 due from the CFGF later in the week, and an annual salary of $5,000, he is sure to get through this tough moment with flying colors.

In the meantime, Bank A gets a phone call from the CFGF shadow bank—there's a problem. The fund that Mr. Hong invested in won't be able to pay the entire sum that was promised upon maturity of the fund. Why? Because Mr. Hong and 9,999 other Chinese were investing their money in a lot of real estate developments in fourth-tier cities. With two property developers unable to sell all the apartments they had prior to completion in cities 4B, 4C, and, more importantly for Mr. Hong, 4A, the CFGF will not receive enough money from the developers to pay back the investors in full. With just five days until the fund matures, CFGF has only $40 million in cash to give back to investors. That is $60 million short of the $100 million maturity payment.

An hour after receiving this news from CFGF, Bank A executives hold a crisis meeting. In the boardroom are the CEO, CFO and key internal team members who were managing the marketing on behalf of CFGF. The tension is high. They hold a conference call with the directors of the CFGF fund and ask for an explanation. The CFGF directors explain that they were part of a syndicate with seven other shadow banks that lent money to three different property developers, and two of those developers have run out of money to complete the construction of multiple apartment complexes throughout cities 4A, 4B and 4C. In addition, their sales were not able to cover the costs for the two property developers to keep on building. Altogether, the two property developers who ran out of money together owed the entire syndicate $600 million. At that moment, because CFGF was the first and only shadow bank to call Bank A, they are now expecting the inevitable. They ask which other shadow banks were involved in the syndicate. They find out that there are ten shadow banks involved in this specific syndicate lending to property developers in Bank A's region of operation, and that there is a good chance that there will be a handful of other shadow banks involved on whose behalf Bank A sells investment products. CFGF breaks the news to Bank A that three of the shadow banks on top of CFGF in the syndicate use Bank A exclusively to raise funds from its deposit holders. Before you know it, the directors of the three other shadow banks call Bank A to inform them of the news that Bank A executives already know.

What was initially thought to be a $60 million problem is now a $240 million problem for Bank A. Why? Because they sold these investment opportunities to their depositors. They told their clients that these were safe financial products to invest in and that they offered great returns on investment. Of course, all this marketing by Bank A on behalf of these shadow banks was done for a fee in the form of commission. What is Bank A going to tell their clients when they come into their offices at the end of the week to discuss their anticipated 100% return on their investment into these shadow bank funds?

The CEO of Bank A calls Beijing and asks the government if there is any possibility that they can get some help to cover the $240 million shortfall. Why would the government do this? To instill confidence that the government is always there to bail out investors who have lost their money investing in shadow banking products. The central government minister tells the CEO of Bank A that there are three other banks from his regions asking for the same kind of help. The CEO of Bank A can safely assume that these have to be the other banks that were raising money for the shadow banks involved in the same syndicate as CFGF—the three shadow banks his bank was working with. The central government minister tells him that they also have a similar problem with a syndicate gone wrong in the northeast and central regions of China. The central government minister advises that they will need a week to figure something out. Unfortunately

Bank A doesn't have a week. Forty-eight hours from now they will be dealing with the bulk of their depositors who invested in the failed shadow banking investments—and Bank A can only offer them $0.40c for every $1 they invested.

The banking system in China has thus far not been tested to this extent. Back in January of 2014, shadow banking companies were put on notice that there would be "no more" bailouts of shadow banking products by the retail banks. Back then, the largest bank in China, ICBC, alongside an undisclosed purchaser, was part of the bailout of a shadow banking product that was called "China Equals Gold No 1." (Who comes up with the names of these funds?) The product cost the bank dearly. Had the ICBC customers of this particular shadow banking product not received full maturity payment and the distressed assets of the shadow bank not been purchased, the shadow banking system would have most probably been sent into an out-of-control spiral.

The CEO of Bank A is feeling the pressure. Bank A has $1.5 billion in cash on its balance sheet, with $40 billion in assets. Like Australian banks, Bank A is already highly leveraged. The CEO and his team will have to make a decision by the end of the next working day. Will they bail out the depositors or will they not? As the CEO of Bank A and his team discuss their options, news breaks of the situation. There is not only the situation in Bank A's region, but there are also two other similar scenarios in China. The three failed shadow banking syndicates throughout the country have close to $1.5 billion that will not be repaid by property developers at maturity, which is in just 24 hours. The moment that the world feared may be just 24 hours away. Like all the other banks that provided similar services to these shadow banks and their depositors, Bank A has the choice to take the hit themselves and bail out the depositors so the money will keep flowing for its competitors, or they have to make the deposit holders take the hit. If the depositors take the hit, there will be a rush of money out of the shadow banking system into the retail banking system. Essentially, what these banks could cause is not a run on the banks, but a run on the shadow banks. Bank A sets up a conference call with the other banks that have been affected by the failed syndicate and they all mutually agree that if they don't pay their depositors the money, mayhem will result. On the flipside, they see themselves as being possibly the first banks to let their depositors take a hit of what could be something worse brewing in the marketplace. If their depositors take the hit now, it will be nowhere near as bad as the hit the depositors will have to take at another bank caused by a rush to pull money out of their competitors' banks.

With the market on edge just twelve hours before the banks open the following day, the CEO of Bank A makes a public statement. "Anyone who invested in the CFGF financial product will only get back 40% of their original investment. I am sorry, but unfortunately not all investments work to plan." All the CEOs of the fellow banks that were involved in this failed investment product relay the same message. This sends the markets into negative territory. It is at this moment that the Chinese property bubble pops. But early the next morning on CNBC, some of the institutional investors that the reporters interview believe that the $3 billion hit to depositors at various banks is not such a big deal relative to the overall size of the Chinese economy and the $7-trillion+ shadow banking system. Some, however, call it the end of the bubble. In this scenario, it is the beginning of the end of the greatest property bubble in human history.

Why is this the end of the greatest property bubble in human history? Because the next morning after the public statement made by the CEO of Bank A, Mr. Hong walks into the local Bank A branch to receive the maturity payment of his investment into the CFGF product and discuss his future. Mr. Hong doesn't have a TV, nor does he listen to radio, so he has not heard the news. The banker says, "I'm very sorry, Mr. Hong, if you have not yet heard the news. The CFGF fund will not be able to pay back 100% of the $10,000 investment you made. All they can offer is $4,000. We will make sure these funds are in your account by the end of the working day." Mr. Hong is in shock. He responds, "But I just bought a property four days ago! I need that $10,000 to get me through the first eight months!" The banker sincerely apologizes to Mr. Hong, but says that unfortunately there is nothing he can do to make things better.

Mr. Hong is having a very bad start to his day. As he's walking out of the bank, other depositors who lost 60% of their investments start to scream at the bankers. It's pretty clear that the frustration is going to send depositors into a rage that may turn violent. Mr. Hong, being the gentleman that he is, doesn't want to be a part of what may be about to happen. He gets on his bicycle and rides back to the construction site. Mr. Hong's bad day is about to get much worse. The construction site manager brings all the workers together to tell them that the construction company that they work for will not continue to build this property because the property developers have run out of money. This is the worst news that poor Mr. Hong could imagine. The property he purchased off the plan will not be built, and $40,000 of his parents' life savings have just been lost. The property developers were one of two property developers that failed to repay the shadow banking syndicate that CFGF was a part of. Mr. Hong and his team members are told that the construction company will now build at a new site for another property developer five miles away, and to be there bright and early the next morning.

Just six hours after waking, Mr. Hong lost 60% of his savings and $40,000 of his parents' life savings. To make matters worse, he still has to pay back to the IMF shadow lender interest and principal on the loan he took out to purchase the apartment that is never going to exist. Mr. Hong goes to talk to the finance specialist who offered him the IMF-backed loan, and explains the situation. The financial specialist says that he needs to go to the local IMF office and discuss his problem, as he does not get involved in, nor cares about, Mr. Hongs bad day and financial situation. Mr. Hong jumps on his bike, heads to IMF's office, and walks through the front door—only to see fifty other property investors who also borrowed money from IMF to purchase an apartment at the now-defunct construction site where Mr. Hong had been working and would one day live. "They said if I paid upfront they would give me a big discount," a woman pleads to a lender as tears fall down her face. Mr. Hong is not the only one who has lost a lot of money.

This scene is systematically replicated throughout the three regions of China where shadow banking syndicates have failed. Not only have a handful of property developers gone bust, but also about 300,000 depositors and 150,000 property buyers are all now affected from the failure of $2 billion in maturity payments. With widespread news of the failure of three large shadow banking syndicates across China, the marketplace becomes incredibly nervous. The central government in Beijing stands by the decision of the affected banks to "not" bail out the depositors who made the choice to take the risk to invest in external banking products when they had the retail bank willing to offer 3% interest.

The effect of this statement by the central government and the fact that investors of a handful of shadow banking products have lost up to 60% of their investment spooks investors to a point where the majority of investors in shadow banking products do not want to invest anymore in their products. In fact, hour after hour, more investors want their money returned to them right away. Shadow banking businesses across China are all hearing the same messages from their investors. There is more than $7 trillion invested in shadow banking products. Of this $7 trillion, the shadow banking industry as a whole has just 3%, or $210 billion, cash on hand. A good proportion of wealthy Chinese individuals and retail banks themselves become nervous and are demanding the return of the money they invested into a particular shadow banking instrument. Each and every shadow bank is trying to buy as much time as they can with investors, because investors across China are demanding the combined return of $800 billion.

Some investors agreed upon signing to lock in their investments for a certain period of time and will not be able to recoup their funds until maturity. But those investors who have not signed such a clause in their investment agreement have the right to ask for their money back. Essentially, the equivalent of 9% of China's total GDP is being demanded by investors to be returned right away. This is simply not physically possible because the shadow banks have lent the majority of this money to property buyers, property developers, and construction companies—and they only have $210 billion in cash. As for Bank A being one of the first banks to send the market in the direction, it is now happy it made the choice to let the depositors be punished for making bad investment decisions—even if the decisions were following Bank A's advice. Why? Because the shadow banking system is in a lot of trouble, and anyone who was smart enough to get their money out of the shadow banking system will keep that money in the registered and official retail banking system. This means more depositors for Bank A. Furthermore, Bank A, being the legitimate bank that it is, will have a better chance of being bailed out by the Chinese government if it needs to be.

Meanwhile, what's happening in China is making news in Australia—but not to the extent it should be. It's not on the front pages of the newspapers, and it's not headlining the evening TV news. But it is making an impact. There is an across-the-board 3% to 4% drop in Australian mining stocks, and the $AUD drops by 1c against the $USD. The overall sentiment by Australian pundits is that it's just another short-term credit problem that the Chinese government will fix over the next several days. They assume the problem will be solved momentarily, so it's not really worth discussing and there's no reason to be concerned. Over at the mining companies, executives call up their sales teams to see if sales are still increasing, but sales are flat. This is of no concern to the miners.

The crummy 2-bedroom home in southern Sydney that went for auction back in Chapter Six of this book is now up for auction again. Since purchasing the property in January 2014, the buyer has fixed the floors, painted the walls and built a new kitchen. It sells for $999,000—$75,000 more than the seller bought it for back in January 2014. Unfortunately, the property investor who won that very intense auction seventeen months earlier has just lost a few thousand dollars, once he calculates all the costs. But overall, the property-price-to-income ratio in Sydney is now 10.3x income. Loan-to-income ratios have now climbed past the 8.1x income mark.

Back in China, only ten days after Mr. Hong lost 60% of his lifesavings and 45% of his parents' life savings, and was left with nothing but a loan of $35,000 to pay off, he has just received more bad news. The new construction site where he and his team were supposed to work will not go ahead because the property developer was not able to secure funding through the shadow banking system. Is Mr. Hong the unluckiest person in China? It feels like it. But the problem in China is getting worse. Steel fabricators across China begin to cancel orders of steel from their suppliers; there has been a sharp drop in the need for steel to build apartment complexes that happened as a result of property developers struggling to get their hands on debt through the shadow banking system. New construction cannot begin unless the property developers are capitalized. With steel fabricators canceling orders, steel suppliers are forced to reduce their need for steel's most valuable ingredient—iron ore. Decreased demand will take another two to three weeks to filter through the supply chain, but in anticipation of reduced demand of iron ore, the spot price moves from $122 per metric ton down to $109.

There is now an incredible standoff between investors and the shadow banking system. Five days earlier, shadow banking product investors as a whole were demanding the return of $800 billion across the shadow banking system. Three days later there is now $1 trillion being demanded by investors. That is almost 5x the amount of cash the shadow banking system has in hand. Essentially, the shadow banks are caught in a situation where they need to pay back 5x more cash than the cash they have in the bank—and no new investors are investing in their financial instruments. What we have here is a shadow banking credit crunch and a run on the shadow banks.

News is spreading quickly, and increasing numbers of investors are demanding their money back. The Shanghai Composite index drops 9% and the Hang Seng index in Hong Kong drops 8%, and secondary effects pass throughout the global markets. By the next day, the Australian Stock Exchange (ASX) is battered by 10%. Why did the ASX take such a battering? Because there's a shadow banking credit crunch in the world's second-largest economy, which pulls investors away from the banking stocks, and because construction is slowing down at a very rapid rate in China, meaning that miners will not be making the same money they did the year before. Because the ASX is weighted heavily on mining and banking stocks, it takes a bigger overall hit. Essentially the moment that some of the world's most famed short-sellers knew would one day happen is coming to fruition right in front of their very eyes. In just twenty-four hours, the $AUD slides another $0.04c and is now hovering around the $0.65c mark against the $USD. The stock markets and currencies that depend just as much on China— such as Korea, Singapore and Brazil—are plunging.

It's now late July, and Australia's largest companies begin to release their financial results. Because of the recent nature of the Chinese credit crunch, the Big 4 banks make record-breaking profits, which helps the ASX recoup some of the losses in recent weeks. The mining companies have yet to feel the true impact of the shadow banking credit crunch in China, and they produce strong profits. But all business leaders are expressing caution for the coming year.

Back in China, the problem is getting worse by the day, and the spot price of iron ore has now dropped below the critical USD$90 per metric ton. But in $AUD terms, the Australian miners can still operate profitably. The Chinese government is trying to figure out how to solve China's shadow banking credit crunch. With investors now demanding more than $2 trillion in funds to be returned, the shadow banking system has effectively hit a brick wall. No money is being returned to investors and no money is being lent. The Chinese central government has a big problem; every day that property developers do not construct cuts into the country's GDP. Worst of all, the assets held by the shadow banks are losing value minute by minute. They have essentially invested $7 trillion in assets, and those assets are now only worth somewhere from $4.5 to $5.5 trillion. How can the Chinese government bail out the shadow banking system? These are essentially off-balance-sheet investments. The government has no clue as to how much money is actually invested through the shadow banking industry. And is the Chinese government going to print $2 trillion to bail out either the informal shadow banks or its investors? Why would the government do such a thing? Because local governments are now running out of cash to operate government services.

The tsunami of bad news in China is now packaged in the form of reality heading at a rapid rate directly toward the second pillar of the Australian economy. The mining companies receive phone call after phone call from their Chinese customers: "Cancel our orders, we don't need anymore iron ore at this point in time." The internal strategy and finance teams at the mining companies start to do the math. In a matter of weeks there is an across-the-board 30% drop in demand for iron ore. And news spreads quickly throughout the financial markets. The credit crunch that was hopefully just a short-term resolvable problem has now become the worst nightmare for any mining company. The spot price of iron ore relentlessly slumps toward USD$30 per metric ton. With the $AUD now at $0.55c against the $USD, the spot price of iron ore has crashed through the break-even point of every mining company in Australia. In just ninety days, the first pillar went from being a highly profitable industry that held the view that they were invincible to an industry hemorrhaging money.

In the meantime, the Big 4 banks have sent their best marketing teams to New York and London on their regular monthly mission to attract more funding from the wholesale lending market. Unfortunately for the hotshots, the market as a whole is asking a lot more questions before lending any money. "Does your bank as a non-government entity have any experience dealing with a credit crunch? How do you expect to recover the funds from mortgage holders if the property market falls as it did in the U.S., Spain and Ireland? How are the mining companies going to pay interest? Why does your bank's balance sheet look like the balance sheet of Lehman Brothers before it went bust?" They then hear, "You Australians learned nothing from the GFC. You're about to have a prime mortgage crisis. Get out of my office!" The once-friendly foreign wholesale lenders now want their money back. They've been through this before. The executives at all the Big 4 now have a real world problem on their hands. Access to debt for the Big 4 has dried up. For years, Australians truly thought that things were "different" in Australia. But reality is setting in with the Big 4's marketing teams that Australia is no different. When the marketing teams return to Australia after getting nothing more than a mouthful from the wholesale lending market, the Australian economy for the first time in almost a quarter century enters a new era— the era where history repeats itself and uses Australia this time as the example.

While the mining companies are now losing a combined $300 million a day, the Chinese government is trying to figure out how to unravel a credit crunch in the informal banking sector. Furthermore, Chinese-purchased new homes across Australia start to be put back on the market. Why? Because there's a good chance that a fair proportion of wealthy Chinese who own property in Australia, indeed around the world, have a cash-flow problem. If they cannot recoup their investments in the shadow banking system in China, they need to get their hands on cash another way. At the same time, to make matters worse, the RBA is now forced to increase interest rates because the $AUD has fallen by $0.30c to the $.60c mark so fast that panic is now settling into the Australian economy as a result of inflation now being at 7%. The RBA has no alternative but to increase the interest rate by 75 basis points. A reserve rate of 3.25% will drive fortnightly home-loan repayments higher across Australia. Although the interest rate is still at a relatively low level, too many Australian property buyers took on as much debt as they possibly could to secure a property when interest rates were at 2.5%. This is the moment that a needle is planted firmly into the great Australian property bubble, and it is a hard moment for Australians to swallow. Over the previous five years, the majority of property buyers purchased their dwellings using 80% leverage on top of high property-price-to-household-income ratios. If you were a household with a $70,000 annual income and a mortgage of $500,000, you now have to pay an extra $72 a week to the bank on top of the inflating prices for goods and services.

With the mining sector taking an absolute beating, the inevitable starts to happen. Five of the largest Australian iron ore suppliers have between two to twelve weeks of cash reserves before they have to declare bankruptcy. The Abbott government, just like the Chinese government, is in crisis mode; they need to figure out a way to soften the blow in Australia. Some of the world's leading private-sector economists from the U.S. and Europe cannot make it any clearer that, "China is going to have to figure out an alternative way to get its economy back up and running. Unlike 2008, China cannot build its way out of this situation. They have built more infrastructure and housing than they will need for the next twenty-five years or more!" Australian diplomats based in China do their best to convince the Chinese government to make some sort of bailout to its economy and shadow banks so that the construction bandwagon can get moving again. "Are you stupid?" the Chinese diplomats tell their Australian counterparts. "We've already built too much! I'm sorry, but we have bigger priorities at the moment than to build more dwellings just to save a mining industry outside our jurisdiction." The Australian government is now experiencing an economic headwind like never before, and for every day with no action, the country is losing billions in asset value because the mining giants are heading toward stock market capitalization of $0. The mining giants plead with the banks to give some flexibility on the hundreds of billions in debts they have to pay back from all the capital expenditure in recent years. The Big 4 have a strong involvement with the mining sector and have been part of many syndicate loans to the sector.

Property prices in China are decreasing by 3% per week. Almost every apartment in City 4A is for sale. Real estate agents cannot find any buyers still willing to pay 50% less than the price of the apartments were at just five months ago. The Chinese government has to take immediate measures to stop the carnage in its economy; 300 million Chinese, both rich and poor, could now lose all their investments in the shadow banking sector—during the time that they've been unable to get their money back from the shadow banking system, the assets the shadow bankers invested in have now lost 50% in value. Essentially there is $7 trillion in cash owed to investors, but the assets the shadow banks hold are only worth $3.5 trillion. With Gross World Product (GWP) at $72 trillion, $3.5 trillion is now lost (5%) and the other $3.5 trillion (5%) is caught between a rock and a hard place in China. The Chinese take the U.S.-style approach and decide to buy $2 trillion in toxic property assets. But where the Chinese take a different approach is that the government will bail out the property owners and the formal banking system, not the shadow banks. To save the entire system would cost $6 trillion (66% of GDP), but that is simply too much money. Even though $2 trillion is an exorbitant amount of money, it is nowhere near enough money—which illustrates the sheer size of the problem in China.

In Australia, the Abbott government realizes that it cannot save the mining industry—it would cost over $100 billion. By October, the spot price of iron ore falls to just USD$18 per metric ton. At this point, practically all miners except for Rio Tinto and BHP call in the administrators and file for bankruptcy. The $AUD is now down to $0.48c against the $USD, and still, inflation has yet to be tamed. The RBA again has no choice, and it brings the reserve rate up 150 basis points. The RBA needs the dollar to climb back to $0.60c or higher to slow down inflation, which is now close to 10%. Unfortunately, this spells bad news for the first and third pillar of the Australian economy. Global attention focuses on the domestic Australian economy, now that the second pillar has essentially collapsed. The RBA governor warns: "Expect interest rates as high as 10% by June 2016." With the Big 4 banks highly exposed to the collapse of three of the five largest Australian mining companies, they essentially have to forfeit half their cash on hand to cover immediate losses. And as the market is completely spooked and unemployment in

Australia has rushed passed 8%, forecasted thresholds are just being ploughed through by this economic disaster. The banks now have to take a hit from the mining sector on top of the wholesale lending markets that have gone completely risk adverse, so they start to tread toward running out of money. They are forced to stop lending because they simply have no money to lend. And while all of this is happening, homeowners are lining up to try to get some leniency on their debts.

The sudden drop in Chinese demand for iron ore has knocked out three of the five largest mining companies in Australia. Now that there are only two iron ore producers in the country, the spot price of iron ore begins to rise slightly day after day. If the spot price of iron ore can climb to USD$30 per metric ton by the end of 2015, BHP and Rio Tinto will survive the greatest financial storm in the industry's history—and all because over the last several weeks it took the drastic measures to spare every cent of cost. The rivals didn't, and they paid the price.

The Abbott government now turns its focus on the banking and housing sectors. Real estate agents have never been busier for the wrong reasons. They all have a record number of listings on their books. But demand is dead. There are hardly any buyers in the property market; nobody has enough cash to buy a house because the banks aren't lending. The Ponzi-style growth scheme of the banks has collapsed. Demand for Australian property, relative to supply, was stimulated by the banks' willingness to lend excessively, and now reality has sunk in. The Australian property market is imploding. Millions of households across the country have had to put their properties on the market at the same time because they cannot afford to pay the interest. The asset value of what Joe Hockey once called a very "different" asset class in 2013 is now steamrolling toward correction territory. And by December 2015, the median house price in Australia's major cities drops by an average of 25%. The balance sheets at the banks are in turmoil, and two of the Big 4 have now run out of cash. The industry as a whole can only survive if there is a government bailout. The Abbott government has no choice. What is clear is the prolonged property bubble that was fueled by a credit bubble has collapsed.

The Big 4 banks are now losing close to $8 billion a month, and WBC and CBA have less than four days of cash reserves. NAB and ANZ can only survive for another two weeks if CBA and WBC fail. Prime Minister Abbott summons the Big 4's CEOs to Canberra to examine the extent of the problem. The CEOs try to convince Abbott for an urgent American-style bailout of the banks, and ask for an immediate $150 billion capital injection into their businesses. But the prime minister is furious with these CEOs. He tells them that Australians have now learned a valuable lesson about taking on too much debt, saying, "Let's hope Australians never forget what happened a week before Christmas of 2015." Of all the Australian industries that cannot collapse, the most important has to be the first pillar of the Australian economy, and Abbott and Hockey know this. Had the banks not made such a huge bet on the property sector and instead diversified their investments, there's a good chance that they would not be in need of government assistance. Abbott and Hockey see that they have two options—they can either bail out the banks like the Americans with an initial payment of $150 billion (and counting), or they can nationalize the Big 4. They have three days before the CBA and WBC become the two largest corporate collapses in Australian history, with a combined $1.3 trillion of assets that would be put under administration. Ultimately, this would also take out NAB and ANZ—making for an absolute catastrophe. Abbott decides to purchase each bank for $1 and nationalize them; it's very clear that the Big 4 needs a whole lot more than $150 billion to get themselves out of the mess they got themselves into.

Now that the Big 4 have been nationalized, one thing is clear—the banks will probably never again be allowed to lend such high leverage ratios to households. This means that property prices can only go one way—down. At least until property price ratios come into reasonable line with median household incomes. As a result, one generation of mortgage owners will be forever underwater. In just six months, the Australian economy declines in GDP by 5%. If this trend continues, Australia will enter depression by June of 2016. Worst of all, apart from the United States, all other major trading partners have been just as affected in ways that might even be worse than the catastrophe of the shadow banking credit crunch in China. Korea, Singapore, Thailand and Indonesia are now entering the early stages of economic depressions. It will take China more than a generation to recover from such a shock to the system—a system that was clearly inflated to a point that just made no sense.

It will take Australia several years to recover from such a shock to the economy. By the time all the accounting is done, the Australian government is probably looking at a $300 to $400 billion write-off just in private sector debts. The government's prospective ability to recoup this shortfall of money from households seems near impossible. The initial shock to the mining sector was too quick and too harsh to rescue. But the government will still try to get Australians to pay off their debts, one way or another.

Over in the United States and Europe, the cost of raw materials has never been cheaper. Although their economies fall into recession, their situations are much milder than the fallout in the Asia-Pacific region. A generation caught up in high steel prices is now free from the ridiculously high costs of steel for a long time. A rebalance of the global economy slowly begins.

Ultimately, Australia will be a big loser from a Chinese shadow banking credit crunch. This hypothetical scenario gives insight into how a chain of external economic-driver events can create a domino effect that rips through the heart of the Australian economy. The national dependency on the mining sector exposes Australia to the economic shocks of a country that has little control over its shadow banking industry. All it takes is a scenario similar to this one to send a domino effect that starts in a fourth-tier Chinese city in China and affects the greater Chinese Economy. Then from China, the dominos fall until they hit the second pillar of the Australian Economy, and then the first pillar, until finally the third pillar is shaken to its core. It's alarming to realize just how interconnected and dependent the first and third pillars are on the second pillar. What's more distressing is that it takes just a $3 billion default to cause a $7-trillion credit crunch that can send shockwaves throughout the world.

The only good economic news that comes out of Australia in this hypothetical period of economic tragedy, is that non-mining exports and manufacturing pick up over the emerging change of economic dynamics. For the first time in years, Australia now becomes a cheaper place to manufacture than the United States and Western Europe. But the problem is that there will be weak demand for anything from Asia for years to come.

This scenario also shows that the Australian economy is no "different" than those of other countries. Bubbles can pop. In this scenario, there is absolutely no possible way Australia could avoid a recession. Whether it could avoid a depression would probably be the more important question. With an economy that completely lacks industrial diversity, there is nothing for Australia to fall back on. Because Chinese growth has been so fast over the prior ten years, it's inevitable that China will face a financial crisis similar to the one in this hypothetical scenario. When the economy of the USSR failed, they were in the middle of a race against the United States for global supremacy. Essentially, the USSR waived the white flag and the Cold War ended. Their command-driven economy could not keep up with the Jones's and eventually failed. China is in a race against itself. That's what is different between the two command-driven economic models. China has grown too fast, too soon—and the faster the rise, faster the fall. That is why in this scenario it only takes a matter of weeks to spark significant concern, and just a matter of months for the Australian economy to feel the secondary effects of a country that spent too much artificial money on growth. In order to keep up with the times, Australia got ahead of itself, and its private sector took on too much debt that was exceptionally exposed to an external shock.

Chapter Ten

Scenario 2:

The Domestic Event that Causes the Knockout of Pillars One and Three

This hypothetical scenario is based on a plausible real-life scenario that could take place based on a domestic shock to the economy.

Scenario Two

It's September of 2015. Unemployment in Australia has risen to 6.7%, and the spring selling season has begun in Sydney. The Taylors are newlyweds with a baby due in seven months. Mr. Taylor is a plumber and Ms. Taylor is a secretary. Mr. Taylor likes to catch up with his mates at the pub every Friday afternoon, and Ms. Taylor loves her trendy, pricy Saturday lunches with her girlfriends. Their annual household income is $95,000 after taxes. They spend $450 a week in rent and have been able to save $95,000 between them over six years. Like most other first-time homebuyers, The Taylors are looking for their small slice of the Australian dream. Both of them have lived all their lives in the Sutherland Shire (The Shire) of Sydney, and their parents and grandparents have always called The Shire home. It's a beautiful part of the world that's forty minutes from downtown Sydney with beaches and waterways at their doorstep.

The Shire is one of Australia's best-kept secrets. Foreign tourists don't generally flock to this part of the city, but they're amazed when they do. In September 2015, the Taylors start to count up their savings and try to figure out how they will be able to afford to buy a house somewhere in The Shire. Their focus is the Shire suburbs east of Miranda. In 1985, Mr. Taylor's parents bought their dream family home in The Shire—$130,000 for their 5-bedroom home in Caringbah South. Mr. Taylor's parents had a household income of $30,000. With a $30,000 deposit, they were able to get a 15-year loan, and by 2000, they had made their final mortgage payment. But times have significantly changed since 1985.

Today, the younger Taylors go to the Big 4 banks to enquire how much they can borrow to purchase a property. A 20% deposit is what each of the Big 4 demands. Mr. and Ms. Taylor do the math and calculate that they can get a loan of $450,000 from any of the Big 4. The banks are offering interest rates that range from 5% to 5.3%. The Taylors decide that the bank offering 5% interest would give them the best deal. After consulting with the banks, Mr. and Ms. Taylor now go property hunting and they realize they have a big problem. There are no houses in the whole Sutherland Shire that are under $800,000. Since the recent modest gains in property value, the properties in the eastern region of the Shire cost now well in excess of $1 million. $1 million won't even get you the most run-down dump that can be demolished with a shoulder charge. As you move further west in the Shire into the Kirrawee and Kareela area, median prices in September 2015 are at $1 million. The Taylors can't believe it. They've saved responsibly and if they were in any other city in the Western world outside of Australia, there's a pretty good chance that for $550,000 they would be able to buy a dream 4-bedroom home in an area comparable to The Shire. (In Houston, it would get you a 4-bedroom masterpiece in the Woodlands, complete with a built-in movie theatre, plus two top-of-the-line Mercedes or Audis to put in the 4-car garage.)

With a baby on the way, the Taylors have to make a choice. Do they decide to move into another neighborhood of Sydney further out west, or do they talk to their parents to get some assistance? First they decide to venture into other neighborhoods further inland in Sydney. The conclusion is very clear: there's not much they can buy with $550,000. After venturing into other neighborhoods, they return home and discuss. They come to the conclusion that they need to ask their parents for help because there is no other way they can purchase a house, even with the most modest of backyards. Mr. Taylor feels the pressure to find a house because he will be a father in seven months, and his wife is making it very clear that she doesn't want to raise the baby in an apartment. Feeling the pressure and the need to secure a house, Mr. Taylor goes back to the Big 4 and to Aussie Home Loans, which is now controlled by the CBA, to ask how other buyers are coming up with such large sums of money to buy housing? The bankers all say to him that, "It's no secret that first-time homebuyers are getting very big helping hands from their parents to get on the property ladder."

Heeding the advice of the bankers, Mr. and Ms. Taylor take their parents for dinner at a nice restaurant in Cronulla overlooking the beach. The in-laws get along great, and they love their children.

More important, the parents have money and equity, and they all have about another ten years left in their careers. Two years ago, Ms. Taylor's parents purchased a modest water-front home in the area, and Mr. Taylor's parents still live in the family home they purchased back in 1985. After some oysters and a lobster platter, Mr. and Ms. Taylor discuss with their parents their intention to buy a home. They tell their parents that they have saved $90,000 and the banks are willing to lend $450,000. They express how they want to live in the local area, and their parents agree that it will take a lot more than $540,000 to find a home. Ms. Taylor's parents are able to help out by giving $60,000 in cash. Mr. Taylor's parents don't have that type of cash, but they offer to put their home up as a guarantee. With $150,000 in cash and a house to be used as collateral, Mr. and Ms. Taylor should be able to purchase a modest 3-bedroom home in the local neighborhood.

By the end of September, the property sections of the newspapers are headlining: "No stopping the property market!" Now one in every four streets in all of Sydney have a median house price of $1 million or higher. Mr. and Ms. Taylor are worried that if they don't buy a place immediately, even the help of their parents will not enable them to buy a modest 3-bedroom home in the local area. They rush their house hunting, and by the first week of October they find two properties that are in the $1 million range. The houses are nothing special, but that is the Taylors' limit. To confirm they have the adequate purchasing power, they decide to go with WBC due to their better home loan rate. They work with the bank to get the groundwork done before they go to the auctions of the two houses. WBC property surveyors value the house of Mr. Taylor's parents at $1.7 million, which is more than enough to cover the entire $200,000 the bank is requesting in collateral. Based on the couple's income, cash deposit, and collateral, WBC says it would be advisable that Mr. and Ms. Taylor spend no more than $1.1 million on a property, but that they can go $100,000 higher if really need be. Mr. and Ms. Taylor sit down and do the math on the liabilities of purchasing a $1.1 million property. It would mean taking on a maximum of $950,000 in debt—in the first year they would pay $47,500 in interest. WBC understands that it's difficult to pay down principal in the first four to five years, so they agree that the Taylors only need to pay $25,000 in principal over the next four years before moving up to $35,000 yearly principal payments by 2020.

Essentially, unless they take on the absolute maximum amount of debt offered by WBC, the budget of $1.1 million means the Taylors can purchase a property for no more than $1.05 million. Because Mr. and Ms. Taylor needs to factor in the $41,000 stamp duty fee, plus extras such as moving in and other upfront fees, the total will be pushed to $1.1 million.

With all the financing in place when needed, Mr. and Ms. Taylor do one final sit down to comprehend what they're getting themselves into. Because they listen to the pundits from the newspapers and banks, they forecast that the worst-case scenario is that the mortgage rate will rise up to 6% sometime in the next several years after they have taken a small bite out of their principal. They ask each other, " Are we going overboard?" But they believe that property prices will only go up, and that what they're doing is just the normal thing that young homebuyers around the world do. Why? Because that's what their friends and parents tell them. After a final look at the numbers, they know that if they purchase one of the two properties they like for $1.1 million including taxes and costs, they will be paying a total of $72,500 in the first year in mortgage repayments. That is roughly 76% of their after-tax income. They agree that what they're doing is "manageable" against their after-tax income. Clearly Mr. and Ms. Taylor, alongside their parents, are taking all the necessary steps possible to assure that they're able to stay in the neighborhood under their own roof.

The second weekend of mid-October is the big day when the two properties that they "kind of" like are going to Auction. The two houses happen to be across the street from each other, right next door to the home of one of Ms. Taylor's closest friends. Both houses for sale boast a fibro exterior alongside an ordinary interior. The Taylors arrive at the auction of the first home, and there is clear interest for this place, including many older-looking potential buyers. This is the more preferable of the two homes that the Taylors would like to purchase. With five minutes to go before the auction starts, the parents of both Mr. and Ms. Taylor arrive to the auction. The Auctioneer does his magic and describes the mediocre house as if it was as amazing as Oprah Winfrey's home. The auction begins. Straight away, several property investors bid the property from $900,000 to $1.05 million. Mr. Taylor puts his hand up. "$1.06 million," he shouts. That takes him above his personal threshold, but two other bidders quickly outbid him. The auction rushes toward $1.15 million, and Mr. Taylor's dad puts his hand on his son's shoulder and says, "It's ok, mate. Let it go." The auction settles at $1.23 million—way outside their budget. There is an aura of sadness among the newlyweds. Mrs. Taylor sees the pain on his daughter's face and says, "You'll get the next house." While tears fall down Ms. Taylor's cheeks, the very stressed-looking winner of the auction walks into the house alongside the agents to get the paperwork done. The real estate agents are very pleased with the result. At that very moment in countless places across Australia, the same occurrence is taking place, leaving a lot of upset first-time homebuyers and a lot of property investors who have probably stretched themselves to be the highest bidder.

An hour passes and the house across the road is now ready for auction. It's a fairly run-down 180m2 house on a 500m2 block of land and a forty-minute drive from downtown Sydney in The Shire. In the eyes of the Taylors, this is it. If they lose this auction, they're out of luck because it's clear to them that property prices are only going up. They're stressed and their parents feel the pain of their children. The auction begins and Mr. Taylor starts the bidding at $850,000. In a matter of ninety seconds the bidding is up to $1.05 million. Mr. and Mrs. Taylor are in despair. Mrs. Taylor father says, "Keep going, I'll cover you." Mr. Taylor bids again at $1.09 million. "It's ok, go up to 1.14," says Ms. Taylor's father. As the bidding approaches $1.14 million, Mr. Taylor's dad says, "I can chip in another $30,000." The tension is high, and with Mr. Taylor's wife looking at him to make the bid, Mr. Taylor reluctantly throws his hand up: "$1.17 million." His gut is telling him he has spent too much. "Do we have any better bid than $1.17 million?" The auctioneer is searching for a higher bidder. Mr.

178

Taylor looks around and can see the onlookers of the auction shaking their heads in disbelief at the high price for such a modest and, quite frankly, run-down house. "Going once, going twice, sold!" Ms. Taylor is as happy as she has ever been and hugs her husband. The parents congratulate their children. They are the proud new owners of a $1.17 million dwelling in much need of a fix up. They walk into the home, are congratulated by the real estate agents on their bidding, and sign the paperwork.

The next morning, Mr. Taylor opens the newspaper to the property section. The headline says, " A sign of first-time homebuyer desperation—bidding $150,000 above reserve." Above the headline is a photo of the new home he and his wife purchased. That has to hurt to know you bid $150,000 more than the reserve price. Once again, his gut is telling him he has paid too much. But his wife is truly excited and calls up all her girlfriends to share the good news. We bought a home! And she's even happier that she'll be living right next door to her best friend, Ms. Johnson. The Johnsons bought their house back in 2011 for $750,000. Their house was in similar shape to the Taylor's newly purchased home. And by mid-2014, Mr. and Ms. Johnson had knocked down their simple home and put a 350m2 double-story kit home on the plot, and they both drive flashy $90,000 cars. Mr. Johnson is an executive who works in downtown Sydney and earns $140,000 annually after tax, while Ms. Johnson keeps the home tidy. And their house looks great! This house has everything you could ask for alongside the flashy sets of wheels in the driveway. At face value, the Johnsons have the life every young Australian aspires to. It cost the Johnsons $500,000 to build their dream home. In all, they have now spent more than $1.25 million on their property and they have $180,000 of auto finesse. Their home mortgage is $800,000, and they owe $115,000 for their cars.

Monday morning arrives and, before going to work, Ms. Taylor's father transfers $150,000 to the account of Mr. and Ms. Taylor—$90,000 more than originally agreed. Mr. Taylor's father transfers $30,000 to the couple's account and signs the paperwork putting his house on the list of collateral. With a transfer of the property title and a $50,000 stamp duty tax, Mr. and Ms. Taylor are now the proud owners of a $1 million+ mortgage. Across the country, irrespective of income, parents are making the relative risk to help their kids get their first homes.

Meanwhile, outside of Australia there is an increasing amount of commentary by financial analysts on what they believe to be the most unmistakable property bubble the West has ever seen—and it's in Australia. Academics and global organizations such as the International Monetary Fund are backing the talk of a chronic property bubble in Australia. But the local pundits keep squashing their claims: "They don't understand Australia! It's different! We have non-recourse lending in Australia! Australia has no property bubble!" Regardless of what the pundits say, by December of 2015, more and more Australians are doing their homework in relation to property prices. For years they have heard the pundits talk and talk with only a handful of local commentators believing that Australia has a credit-backed property bubble. But the voices of these few commentators have, for one reason or another, not been heard. Their arguments regarding why Australian real estate is in a bubble have been ignored—until now. By December of 2015, the median home price in Sydney hits $910,000. And across Australia the median-house-price-to-income ratio averages out at 7.8 versus 6.7 in 2013. In Sydney, the new-loan-to-household-income ratio has now surpassed 9.1. And the Taylor family is just a few months away from welcoming their first child into the world.

February 2016 arrives, and so do the financial results for the Big 4—predictably as ever, they all post record profits. Why? Because they have Mr. and Mrs. Taylor and every other new homeowner paying more for property than buyers paid last year, and they're willing to lend $1 million to a married couple that has $95,000-after-tax income because the family was able to come up with an equivalent 20% down payment on their property and some collateral. In comparison, in 2006, the median price for property in the United States "peaked" at $USD247,500. This was just shy of 5x the median household income. As a proportion of Australians start to do their research, one thing becomes very clear—the news they have been reading by the pundits has missed a key factor. This is illustrated in the fact that even if every new American homebuyer had taken on a 0% down payment (which was not the case) on their mortgage in 2007 just before the bubble popped, they would've been, on average, still remarkably less exposed to debt than an Australian homebuyer who needs 20% collateral. Apart from the small handful of people skeptical about the Australian real estate market, no Australian property analyst or wholesale lender to Australian banks has ever done the simple math related to the toxic risks that Australian banks and homeowners have made.

As more and more people skeptical of the Australian property market arise, the real estate pundits become more pressured to prove that Australia is not experiencing a long-brewing property bubble. Over at the Big 4 banks, there is evidence that unemployment is making a slight impact to their business models. The evidence is that the mortgage default rate is climbing due to 150,000 Australians having lost their jobs in the last twelve months. Roughly 9% of these people took on a mortgage over the last four years and are now unable to pay interest or principal. But in February of 2016, the banks don't seem concerned, as they are able to sell properties at a higher price than the value of the mortgages owed, covering their risk. From this point on, Australians will never view real estate as an investment in the same way again.

In March of 2016, a major business in Australia that employs tens of thousands of Australians across the country falls into bankruptcy. The company cites that high wages and high cost of doing business in Australia made its business entirely uncompetitive in the global marketplace. Within an instant, 35,000 jobs are directly lost to the bankruptcy. Over the coming weeks, another 40,000 jobs will indirectly be lost, as the suppliers of this large bankrupt company have lost their prime source of revenue. Because the employees of the bankrupt company are predominantly unionized, wages are high. Around 12,000 of these employees have purchased a property in the last four years; of these homes, 90% were purchased using 80% leverage. Without any income, many of the bankrupt company's former employees are forced to sell their dwellings, and fast.

The failure of this bankrupt company has a huge impact on the greater Australian economy. The $AUD weakens against the $USD, dropping down to $0.79c in just three weeks after the bankruptcy. In an instant, the cost of imported goods rise, which puts a smile on the face of the mining executives. With the spot price of iron ore hovering around the $USD98 mark, the profitability of the mining industry is improved. Furthermore, it seems that the Chinese economy is still attempting to go for growth and will be purchasing significant quantities of iron ore relative to output for at least another nine to twelve months. And as for the United States, it has now ended its QE program. To everybody's immediate surprise, the anticipated negative impact on the American and global economy has been small.

While mining companies and other exporters feel the positive effects of the weaker $AUD, the general public feels the adverse effects. Inflation is rising. The RBA and the Australian government made a big bet on the third pillar of the Australian economy to pull the country away from its dependency on the mining industry; unfortunately, it has come at a significant cost. Australian households were already chronically overleveraged back in 2013—more than any other Western country relative to household income and in relation to the entire sum of the loan. With volatility in the currency market, foreign investors have become concerned about investing their money in Australian assets. On the domestic side, new homebuyers have been stretched beyond all reasonable logic.

By May of 2016, with corporate Australia now struggling with more job losses, more newly unemployed Australians with an outstanding home loan equivalent to 4x income or higher are forced to put their properties on the market. Within a matter of months, there are twice as many homes for sale as there were back in spring of 2015. The pundits still insist there is no concern about a bubble popping, but data suggests otherwise. Property prices have stalled. To make matters worse, properties are not exchanging hands. Sellers with outrageous mortgages are trying to sell their properties to recoup the entire amount they owe their bank.

As with the previous scenario, news spreads quickly that trouble seems to be brewing in the mighty Australian property market. And the Big 4 banks are struggling to raise money to keep their business model running smoothly. Why? Because if the banks loan less to homebuyers than they did the year before, they cannot increase their profitability, and this has the potential to send the market valuation of these banks very quickly tumbling down. Alongside continuous increase in default rates, banks are still able to recoup their investments.

With property prices stagnant, inflation rising quickly and banks struggling to find the money to lend to new homeowners, the credit-backed, Australian real estate bubble enters unchartered waters. With inflation now at 4.1%, the RBA has no choice but to stem inflation. The interest rate rises by 0.25% and the average variable home loan increases to 5.5%. With fear of coming interest rate hikes, more highly leveraged homeowners and property investors have to put their properties on the market. And before you know it, there are 15,000 extra homes for sale in Sydney with similar increases in available housing stock relative to scale across Australia.

The Taylors will now pay an extra $2,500 a year in interest. They had never forecast that interest rates would rise so quickly, and their incomes have little room for error. Their parents have a little bit of spare cash left after the deposit, and they pitch in by paying $3,000—or half a month's mortgage payment. This will cover the increased mortgage payment. Mr. and Ms. Taylor are relieved, but they agree they are going to have to change their lifestyle in order to be able to comfortably pay off this highly leveraged mortgage relative to their incomes. Ms. Taylor doesn't want to give up her lunches with her girlfriends, including her neighbor and best friend, Ms. Johnson.

In June of 2016, Mr. Johnson returns home to tell his wife that he has lost his job. While the Taylors are having dinner in their kitchen, they can't help but hear their neighbor and friend Ms. Johnson screaming at her husband. "How are we going to pay the mortgage?" she screams. Ms. Taylor knows her friend very well. Ms. Johnson doesn't work, and she has enjoyed life as a homemaker—not to mention the finer things in life. On Mr. Johnson's $140,000 salary, he was able to pay his home mortgage down to $665,000 and his auto loans down to $97,000. He has $25,000 in savings to survive on.

A few mornings later there is a "For Sale" sign in front of the Johnson's house. Mr. Taylor sits his wife down and says, " Honey, we need to make more money if we want to keep our home." If interest rates go up another quarter percent, the Taylors are in serious trouble. With a baby in hand, the costs are stacking up. Diapers and other baby costs are taking an extra $190 a week out of their pockets. Mr. Taylor is lucky, being a plumber. Toilets break down all the time. He asks his boss if he can also work an extra weekend shift. Unlike his day shift, he wants to work the nightshift, which means his boss will have to pay extra. His boss is reasonable, and Mr. Taylor has been a hard-working employee for more than five years. "Ok, mate, take the 9pm to 5am Saturday shift." The extra $200 for this shift will make the world of difference for Mr. and Ms. Taylor.

In late July of 2016, and two weeks before the Johnson's home goes up for auction, out in front of the driveway, one of the new $90,000 cars seems to have discretely been replaced by a 2008 Toyota Corolla. And there is more bad news coming hot off the press. "Unemployment continues to rise." It's now standing at 8.2%, and this is enough to send shockwaves throughout the Australian economy. The $AUD dives to $0.70c, leaving no alternative for the RBA; they raise interest rates another 0.25%, and the average home loan rate is now at 6%.

Auction day arrives for Mr. and Ms. Johnson. They owe around $800,000 for their home mortgage, car loan and credit card debt, but they really believe they can sell their house for $1.4 million. Their intention is to pay off their debts and recoup $600,000, which will be their financial lifeline. The real estate agent understands Mr. Johnson's situation. He advises that his real estate agency has noticed an unusual surge in housing stock for sale but that buyers are dwindling. The agent suggests setting the reserve at $1.2 million to be on the safe side so that the house sells. "I want $1.4 million," says Mr. Johnson. The real estate agent agrees to disagree with Mr. Johnson. "The Taylors paid $1.2 million for their piece of rubbish," says Mr. Johnson. The agent reluctantly sets the reserve price for the house at $1.4 million. The auction begins, there are a lot of people at the auction, and the first and last bid is—$900,000. Everyone is either too spooked to buy, or they can't get as much debt as they could when interest rates were lower. The auctioneer is asking if there are any more bidders. Inside the house, the Johnsons are shaking their heads. They need to sell the house or the bank will take it from them. The stress is excruciating.

Mr. and Ms. Taylor are watching the auction. Mr. Taylor's gut is rumbling. If the Johnsons can't get a bid better than $900,000, they don't know what they'll do if they end up in the same situation. With $900,000 as the first and only bid, the real estate agents asks the Johnsons if they want to proceed with the sale, even though it's $500,000 under the reserve price. Mr. Johnson decides to make a vendor bid for $1.2 million and see what happens. "Ladies and gentleman we have a vendor bid for $1.2 million, can anyone go higher," the auctioneer tells the crowd. The auctioneer looks to the individual who made the $900,000 bid, who says, "Not in this market." The property eventually is passed in with a vendor bid of $1.2 million—$300,000 higher than the only bid by the only interested party. The same story is seen across Australia, more particularly in Sydney and Melbourne. Preliminary Auction clearance rates in Sydney and Melbourne both slump to below 50%. By the time all auctions are counted, only 33% of properties have sold. All at a significant discount to what would have been paid for the same dwelling nine months earlier. This news surges across the country; for the first time, property prices begin to decline significantly. Starting in January of 2016, property prices drop 7% across the nation. The reason they haven't dropped further is that sellers like Mr. Johnson are not willing to let their houses sell for less than the price they want. The property market is stalling.

The spring selling season arrives in September of 2016, and there are more properties on the market than ever before. But the spring selling season this year is "different" due to the growing number of foreclosures. Anyone who has lost a job over the last several months has either had to sell property at a discount, or surrender the property to the bank if the property can't be sold. The Big 4 now have a problem. The interbank lending market is not as willing to offer the Big 4 credit. It's starting to become more expensive for the Big 4 to acquire any form of credit, and they have depositors demanding more interest. This causes the banks to seek more guarantees from potential new mortgage customers. Furthermore, the banks have no option but to focus more attention on the default rate of mortgage lenders. In order to improve the risk profile of the assets the Big 4 have on their balance sheets, they have to demand a minimum of 40% deposit from new mortgage holders. There are few alternatives for the banks. Why? **Their business models are now broken. No matter what strategies the banks take, there will be significant pain.** The banks are not able to lend more than they did the year before. Property prices are dropping. And the banks are now forced to take cash out of their own bank accounts to cover the shortfall from the mortgage defaults. Fundamentally, it's all downhill from here.

By November of 2016, WBA and CBA are running at a loss, and NAB and ANZ are not too far behind. Even though the Big 4 banks have built their cash stockpiles to the total tune of $120 billion over the last two years, the defaults are causing more pain than they had anticipated, and they begin to try to sell the foreclosures for less to recoup the entire sum of the failed mortgages so they can repay their creditors—the banks depositors, wholesale lenders and bond holders. With higher interest rates and changing momentum toward investing in real estate, there is only one way the banks can go, and that is down. The banks are still just as leveraged (give or take a few percentage points) as Lehman Brothers was fifteen months before it went bust and all bets were on house prices going up; the Big 4 are caught in the worst possible scenario. But they never thought they could get stuck in this situation; no, they thought Australia was "different." The banks are now priced out of the wholesale lending market, foreign lenders no longer want to lend any money whatsoever to the Big 4, and the rating agencies drop their credit ratings across the board. The only access to credit the Big 4 have is between themselves. NAB and ANZ are the two banks that are just a little less leveraged than WBC and CBA.

By December of 2016, it has become nasty. And although the property market is tumbling, greater focus is now aimed directly at the banks and their balance sheets. With one quarter of negative growth in Australia, it's all but certain that Australia will enter a deep recession. Why? Because the Australian government, the RBA, the banks and the Australian population placed the biggest bet in Western history on property prices going up—just like the Japanese, Irish, Americans and Spaniards before them. And just like these already-failed markets, access to credit has now become hard to come by.

But Australian households have more leverage relative to incomes and by the total sum, because the banks stretched themselves by "toxic" lending—particularly to the Sydney and Melbourne markets, where property prices have dropped 25%. If property prices in Sydney drop 25%, it is essentially the beginning of the end. The average loan size in Sydney is far greater than in any other Australian city or region. Sydney is no New York or London; it has no industry that the city can concretely fall back on other than real estate and domestic banking. And those who are struggling the most with debt are the more recent acquirers of mortgages. In just twelve months, the momentum has gone from "get in now or you will never get into the property market" to "if you are nearly underwater on your mortgage, you sell now or go underwater on your debts." The line has been crossed where the banks need 40% deposit from homebuyers, which wipes out nine out of every ten prospective buyers seeking a single home back in 2013. For the first time in almost a quarter of a century, it's a buyers' market. But there are no buyers.

And as for Mr. and Ms. Taylor, with interest rates continuously rising, they truly have a sad ending. Unlike the Johnsons, who defaulted on their mortgage and lost just the home they owned alongside their dignity, the Taylors have lost a lot more. Because prices have tumbled so much, the banks need to find a way to recoup the debt from the Taylor couple, and Mr. Taylor's parents' property that was used as collateral for the mortgage is now in the hands of the banks.

It's clear that the banks will lose billions, and finally all the warning signs of a credit crunch are upon

190

Australia. When the Big 4 post their financial results in February of 2017, the losses are just staggering—a combined loss of $35 billion in the previous six months alone. The big bet on real estate is now taking its toll. As the headlines say: "Toxic Lending hits Australia." The real estate and banking pundits—who were once the respected commentators that the public truly depended on—are now Public Enemy #1. In the United States and Europe, top banking executives can't believe that the Australian banks did not learn from the challenges they faced in the GFC.

Meanwhile, Pillar Two of the Australian economy could not be happier. Why? Because the domestic Australian economy has taken such a beating that the currency is now below $USD0.50. With the Chinese still seemingly and somehow aiming to build an apartment for every man, woman and child, the iron ore spot price is at $USD90 per metric ton. In $AUD, that equates to $180 per metric ton. They're making a fortune.

It is March of 2017. The stock market is sending the banks toward a market valuation of $0.00 and the balance sheets of CBA and WBC are now showing that within the next several weeks the shortfall between the amount of assets ($1.5 trillion) they have versus what they owe to creditors will be significantly more than the available cash they will have on hand. This sends yet another shockwave throughout the Australian economy. As in the first scenario, if the Abbott government doesn't step in, the CBA and WBC will have to declare bankruptcy. The very fear of this possibility sends depositors into a panic, and there is a run on the banks and the line to deposit money into U.S. and European banks stretches as far as the eye can see. If the CBA and

WBC go bust, they will be the second- and third-biggest bankruptcies in global history—and the NAB and ANZ will inevitably fall too. And with combined assets of the two banks totaling $1.5 trillion (100% of Australian GDP), the problem is of magnetic proportion. As in the previous scenario, the Big 4 seek a bailout from the Abbott government. The difference in this scenario is that the mining industry is still intact for the time being. But it is inevitable that the Chinese will get caught up in their own credit crunch sooner rather than later.

The RBA and the government are given no alternative. They agree to nationalize the banks and print enough money to make a $300 billion bailout with the possibility of printing up to $500 billion. This should hopefully be more than enough money to cover the banks' losses and guarantee the safety of depositors' money. But this comes at a huge cost to the value of the Australian dollar, the cost of foreign debt obligations, and Australia's credit rating.

Over time, property prices moderate as the median price reaches the historic ratio levels. Practically across the board, there is 50% drop in property prices. The belief that Australia is different is squashed, and the public seeks a lot of answers from the government and the RBA—and I'm guessing that a few of those real estate and banking pundits are also on the unemployment line.

Although I am more confident that the demise of the Australian economy will be triggered by a downturn in China, there is always the possibility that a domestic trigger could also lay a similar blow to the Australian economy sans the involvement of the mining sector.

Although the two scenarios discussed are among a multitude of possible scenarios that can stop the Australian economy in its tracks, they are probably the most likely to occur, due to the Australian economy's overwhelming dependency on the second and third pillars. The first pillar has toxic lending practices that will be at the center of any instability, and with such high exposure it cannot navigate out of any economic storm that reaches Australian shores.

What alarms me most about either scenario is the amount of suffering that it will cause families— particularly situations where parents stepped in to help their children get a start on life. Imagine in this hypothetical scenario what it would feel like to be Mr. Taylor and watch the bank take from your parents the home you grew up in because you couldn't pay the mortgage on your own home. It's a shame when good intentions are punished. But on the flipside, it's a clear illustration of how bad it can get when a society becomes married to the belief that property prices only go up. Add to the mix a credit-fueled property bubble that is the most disproportionate in Western history relative to household income, and this scenario could be, and in my opinion, a truly devastating moment for many Australian families. One just has to do the math to comprehend that parents are playing a big role trying to secure dwellings for their children. If the Taylors were living in Houston and they had a $USD82,000 deposit, they could have secured a $140,000 loan and purchased a dream home. Excluding a small handful of places in the world—such as Monaco, Hong Kong and Central London—parents should not be needed to help their kids get into $1 million of debt.

My main point of frustration in both scenarios is that Australians, the three pillars, the Australian government, and the RBA, all have history serving as an example of what happens when there is toxic lending in a country. It seems that nothing was learned from the GFC or that which happened to the Japanese economy. To truly believe things are "different" in any country is the most damaging mentality a nation can have when it comes to economics. The Australian society made a choice not to learn from the mistakes of others. And I do not know why not. We may not be the smartest, but we certainly can't be the dumbest—can we?

Living in The Shire, I see more than my fair share of households that are holding significant debt. "Everyone in The Shire is cashed up [Has lots of cash on hand], Lindsay!" That's what I am always told by the locals. But when you talk to the retail, business, commercial and investment bankers in and around Sydney, you hear a much different story. Yes, there are a handful of people in The Shire with seven-figure bank accounts; but the reality is that the extent of risk the absolute majority of homebuyers have taken on in order to invest or live in The Shire, and across the greater Sydney area, is simply staggering. Yes, the lifestyle is incredible, but I believe that the cost of property is completely unjustified—and the data backs the fact that, beyond a shadow of a doubt, there is a credit-fueled property bubble in Australia.

Chapter Eleven

How Bad Does it Get?

Once again, I do not have a crystal ball. What I do know—based on my research, history and experience working throughout the GFC—is that when the Australian credit bubble pops, the situation will not be good. What makes matters worse for Australia is that today's level of credit in the market related to household incomes is probably the highest ever seen by an entire Western country with a population greater than 1 million. Think about it—23 million people and $1.9 trillion in private sector debt.

Australia will not be sent back to the Stone Age. But historically, in situations like this, the market generally aims toward returning to long-term trend levels. Sydney has a long-term property-price-to-household-income ratio of 5x. When the Australian credit and property bubble pops, Sydney residents will probably expect that over time the property to-household-income ratio will return to 5x from 9x or higher. The same applies for the other cities and regional towns in Australia. But experiencing a declining property market is not easy. As with both hypothetical scenarios in Chapters Eight and Nine, default has matured in all pillars of the economy. Unfortunately, unlike the U.S.—where property owners could return the keys to the bank and let them deal with the problem—in Australia the mortgage holder is stuck with the debt. Pundits believe that this is a good reason why the property prices in Australia won't go down. But when bubbles pop, they are discriminate economic events that do not care whether a mortgage holder has non-recourse debt obligations or not. When a credit bubble bursts and banks start to run out of cash, the law of economics doesn't see the difference between a balance sheet of an investment bank named Lehman Brothers and an Australian retail bank named the CBA. If a bank's balance sheet looks extraordinarily leveraged, you can safely assume that it is.

Can it get as bad as the hypothetical scenarios?

How do I put this? The two hypothetical scenarios in Chapters Eight and Nine are just that—hypothetical. But I use these two hypothetical examples as an illustration of what can happen based on the research I have done and available data. Unfortunately, unlike the pundits, I have history on my side. What alarms me about Australia is that its economy is simply not prepared for a shock. The balance sheets of the banks are too dependent on Pillars Two and Three. I will fall short of saying that the Australian banks are running a Ponzi-style scheme; what I will say is that the banks' business model cannot absorb any pain. It either grows or goes bust. The banking system in Australia is exceedingly leveraged and has no margin for error. So, yes, it is possible that at least one bank will either go bust, or be bailed out or nationalized by the Australian government if property prices fall across Australia to somewhere between 15% to 20%.

What is also clear is that a lot of Australians have made their investment decisions based on flawed data. At worst, decisions were made on hyped-up talk of demand. Data is data and talk is talk. Unfortunately, as in most cases, realization of flawed data only arises once it's too late. One just has to look back at the GFC and Bernard Madoff. It would have been near impossible for anyone to uncover his Ponzi scheme if there had not been a correction in the markets. That correction happened—and what was uncovered was a Ponzi scheme.

Australia has been free of recession since 1991. A lot can happen in twenty-three years, and in Australia, a lot has happened. Australian households have become the most leveraged households in the Western world by sum and any financial ratio you can think of. It is highly problematic when there is flawed data alongside pundits' influence over public opinion. It's almost inconceivable how dependent the domestic Australian economy is on just these two pillars. And because Pillars Two and Three are so interconnected with credit and toxic lending, a correction becomes more savage to an economy. For example, imagine the price of oil dropping and an oil-rich country where banks lend excessively to oil and gas companies. If the oil companies cannot pay back their debts, that's it. It's bust! The banks will never see their money again and they will go bust.

Mining is the only industry the Australian economy has to fall back on if there's a credit crunch or a collapse in property prices. But the mining industry doesn't impact uniformly across the Australian economy. For years we have heard that Australia is a country with two economies: the mining economy and the economy of everything else.

So, yes, when either the Chinese realize they have overbuilt, or Australians realize that property prices are irrationally overpriced beyond belief, you can comfortably assume that the Australian economy will falter. With no new industries in the pipeline to grow significantly over the next few years, there is no chance the Australian economy can save itself from an inevitable bust. This is because when there are only three big industries (all of which have too much leverage geared toward them), history is unfortunately destined to repeat itself.

There is a lot of talk in Australia of wealthy Chinese and other foreign buyers snapping up too much local real estate. I don't believe this is the reason property prices climb in Australia. Before the Japanese went bust, there was talk that they were buying up as much as they could in the state of Queensland. When the Japanese went bust, they disappeared. But they didn't have a real impact on the property valuations, apart from in a handful of suburbs and regions across the state of Queensland. And when the Chinese economy one day faces reality, you will see the influx of Chinese buyers disappear quite quickly. If the foreign buyers of Australian real estate stopped purchasing property tomorrow, it would not pop the Australian property bubble. But toxic lending by the Big 4 to Australian households will. The pundits say the Chinese and other foreign nationals are driving up property prices. They are not. Toxic lending to Australian households is driving up the cost of real estate.

When the Australian property bubble eventually bursts, it will be a very tough moment in the history of Australia. A lot of pride and self-belief that Australia is "different" will unfortunately be squashed. Australians are very proud people. Worst of all, many households and individuals will be very embarrassed. When a bubble pops, it's easy to see who's struggling and who is not simply by the visibility of the "For Sale" signs posted on the front lawns. As it was in the U.S., Spain, Japan and Ireland, people, friends and family will drive past your house and see the sale sign on your lawn that symbolizes your financial hardship. The sign is there for everyone to see and talk about behind your back.

The Australian government will be the savior of the day. If it weren't for the frugal management of the economy during the Howard/Costello era, Australia would have had a lot more public sector debt. The bursting of the Australian private sector credit bubble will cost the Australian government hundreds of billions of dollars. This is where the government has the capacity to absorb private-sector collateral. But doing so doesn't happen quickly; it will take time. When Lehman failed in the U.S., it took another several months for the stock markets and property prices to level off. In the U.S., property prices for a short period fell below the historic average relative to incomes and then returned to the historic levels in most cities and towns. If that happens in Australia, it will shave 50% of value off the property market and leave a generation of homebuyers forever in debt. As mentioned, recessions are very discriminate; they attack those who are the most exposed to debt. Household debt in Australia is so high that it is navigating through unchartered waters. No Western economy has been tested with property and leverage ratios that are so high relative to income across an entire country. It is this that leads me to believe that Australia will most probably take a worse hit than the American economy did back in the GFC. When there is more leverage in the system, there is more room to fall. And the Australian economy has no floor to fall on. We simply do not know how bad it can get. What happened in Spain or Ireland would probably be a better indication of what could happen to the Australian economy—and it's not pretty. Unemployment at 15%+. Youth unemployment at close to 40%. Falling median household income. Banks unable to lend for one to three years. Lack of foreign direct investment. Generations of family wealth wiped out. These are all realities that come with the end of toxic lending.

The world becomes cheaper for a very few. Those who have no mortgage and aren't dependent on property prices rising or the mines still needing more human resources will see a change in their cost of living—it will actually go "down." Cheap property will be in abundance and plumbers and gardeners will be willing to work for less due to a decrease in the number of homeowners who hire them. There aren't many Australians who can be considered "cashed up." But for those few, their world becomes cheaper and their bargaining power becomes incredible.

A market-driven pop of an economic bubble makes the nation look to lay blame on someone. The RBA will probably become the political scapegoat, and probably rightly so due to their failure to manage interest rates. Credit crunches occur when there is too much debt already in the marketplace and not enough to give out. Australia has a private sector debt that is 20% higher than the country's GDP. As mentioned in Chapter Four, when a country has too much debt in its private sector, there is less room to navigate when times get tough. The ultimate question to any central bank when a credit bubble pops and takes down an economy is, "Why didn't the central bank see this coming?" The problem is that over the last several years, the RBA has been managing a credit-driven asset bubble, not an economy. This has been happening for years. Who in their right mind would try to send Australian households toward a loan-to-household-income ratio of 7x to 10x to cover the shortfall from the mining sector? That would just be insane. There is no other way of putting it. But this is what the RBA has done. They dropped interest rates too soon, which influenced more Australians to leverage their lives away to purchase a piece of the most inflated real estate market in modern Western history. You wonder if the RBA chairman has ever actually traveled overseas? Did anyone do any research on historic events that have popped credit and property bubbles?

The credit-driven property bubble is now beyond repair. Even if the RBA chairman wakes up tomorrow morning and decides to set a limit on minimum deposits or leverage ratios that a household can take, it's simply too late. This should have been done ten years ago. Whatever those who run the RBA do from now on, they are dammed if they do and dammed if they don't. If they raise interest rates, the country will plunge into a recession and the public will be outraged; if they lower interest rates, they will invite more new homebuyers to go on toxic lending sprees. It will take Australian wages fifteen to twenty years and no property-price growth to save the Australian property market. But the lack of property growth could be enough to send the Big 4 into a spiral. Remember, the banks need to give out more debt than they did the year before for their business models to function; anything else is a big mess for them. And the RBA allowed the banks to lend excessively to households. Nothing has been done to stop toxic lending in Australia.

If China reduces its dependency and need for iron ore, the smaller mining companies with higher cost structures will start to feel the pinch. Furthermore, miners such as Fortescue Metals offer lower-grade-quality iron ore versus Rio and BHP, which leaves them highly exposed to shocks in the market. But overall, the damage to the mining industry could be apocalyptic. Like the first and third pillars, the mining sector has stretched itself. If the domino-effect scenario unfolds, it could leave the nation with a lot of needless holes in the ground that the mining sector spent hundreds of billions to dig and develop. Imagine $500 billion in fixed investment going to waste in a country with a GDP of $1.52 trillion. Worst of all, there are debts to pay—a lot of them. Defaults on loans by the mining sector will be significant. In order for BHP and Rio Tinto to stay alive in a domino-effect scenario, they will need the right mix of 1) a declining currency and 2) competing miners collapsing sooner rather than later in order to reduce total output of iron ore. The sooner mining companies start to collapse, the sooner the spot price of iron ore moderates due to less production. But the spot price of iron ore has to decline to a point where BHP and Rio Tinto are at least breaking even but their competitors are losing money. This is highly unlikely. All mining companies will suffer significant losses, and BHP and Rio Tinto will just have to try to ride out the storm. It will not be easy, but my calculations say that it is possible.

The secondary effect of a domino event taking place would be much more severe than an internal implosion of the Australian economy. Why? Because the secondary effect brings all three pillars to their knees, leaving the Australian economy with absolutely nothing to fall back on. Towns once populated with miners will become ghost towns. More Australians will be competing against each other for the jobs that Australians were once unwilling to take. At least in the internal-implosion scenario, there is still the ability for the Australian economy to export something of value. However, inevitably, the Chinese will eventually bring to a halt its investment in real estate developments and infrastructure.

Based on historical evidence of credit-backed property bubbles of the past, one thing is clear: It takes years or even decades for an economy to recover when these bubbles pop. Look at Japan. That country still has yet to fully recover from its economic collapse a quarter of a century ago. No matter how hard the Japanese try through stimulus packages and economic incentives, Japan just can't get its economic engine steaming. Ireland and Spain were smashed by the GFC. And in the United States, any property market that buyers were told were "different" took a beating—and those cities and towns were punished for it. From the Midwest to California, carnage was king. Los Angeles was one of the worst-hit cities with its leverage-to-household-income ratios having shot through the roof like they have in Sydney and Melbourne. Property prices fell by almost 50% in some parts of the city. Miami was not far behind L.A. In 2006, Miami property prices peaked at 7x household income. By the end of 2010, prices had dropped to 4x incomes. Still, new homeowners in Sydney are more leveraged relative to household income than the household price-to-income ratio of Miami.

Why does this book focus on Sydney a lot more than it does the rest of Australia? Because Sydney is by far the most credit-backed exposed property market in Australia, and it has the most to lose. Melbourne is not far behind. Their property markets are clearly in a speculative state. Yet these cities don't have the unique characteristics you'd find in the profile of a city that would justify overwhelmingly high property prices. Remember, Geneva has a population density that is more than thirty-two times that of Sydney. The dwelling price in the immediate center of Geneva is about 20% higher than in Sydney, but once you drive ten kilometers from the city center, the price of a dwelling per square meter is lower than that of the greater Sydney metropolitan area. You know something is expensive when the Swiss think something is expensive. And unlike Sydney, Geneva is a small, compact and exceedingly wealthy city. Plus, you have the United Nations and other global organizations clustered in with private bankers and their rich depositors living alongside each other.

Sydney spreads out as far as the eye can see. Australian cities are generally spread out like Texan cities. Miami's greater metropolitan area spreads north to south as far as Sydney does. But Metropolitan Miami doesn't venture inland like Sydney does. If L.A. and Miami property markets can go bust, there is no doubt that Sydney's property market can go bust alongside the other major cities in Australia. Just like Miami and L.A., Australia's property boom has been driven by toxic access to credit. Miami and L.A. are slightly denser than Australian cities, and home sizes are fairly similar to the homes in Australian cities. More tourists flock to Miami and L.A. than to any city in Australia. These U.S. cities have big economies. The GDP of Los

Angeles itself is almost 50% of the entire GDP of Australia. Los Angeles suffered through the GFC, and even eight years after property prices peaked, prices have yet to fully recover (inclusive of the increase in household incomes over the six years since the GFC hit). But it must be noted that property prices in L.A. today are on the rebound and are moving rapidly, igniting fears of another property bubble. This is not what Australian cities will most likely experience. The road to recovery in Australia will be longer, and credit will be much harder for households to access for a very long time.

Look at the following table. City A is a relatively close example of what median Sydney homebuyers face in terms of taking on debt and the proportion of their income required to service debt versus the general cost to purchase a property in other Western countries. Just because you need to put more money down as a deposit, doesn't mean it's easier to pay off the mortgage. The after-tax income of City A is 50% more than that of City B, but City A's inhabitants shouldn't pay 5x the price for a property. When a credit crunch arises, the banks investing in City A will find themselves in a much harder position to recoup their debts, because the asset valuations have a lot more room to fall and mortgage holders need to give their creditors a bigger chunk of their incomes. This is what can happen to Australian cities. Think of the damage to the Australian economy as property prices drop to a point where they become relative to City B and C versus household income.

City	A	B	C
Household incomeAfter-tax)	$75,000	$50,000	$40,000
Median property price (including stamp duty)	$750,000	$150,000	$200,000
Minimum deposit required	20% or $150,000	0% or $0	10% or $20,000
Average loan amount	$600,000	$150,000	$180,000
Loan size vs. income ratio	8	3	4.5
Interest Rate	5%	4%	3%
% of income going to mortgage repayments	72%	24%	31.5%

As per the above, if you were a wholesale lender seeking low-risk investment (which most banks seek), where would you prefer to send your money to be invested into home loans? Can you trust that new homebuyers of City A will be able to pay off their debts as easily as City B or C? No. And when the wholesale lending market retracts its position on a specific housing market that already holds an incredible sum of leverage per household relative to incomes, less money enters the financial system and slows things down. Less debt available in City A equates to fewer buyers able to purchase a home. And that is why both scenarios in Chapters Eight and Nine suggest that the Big 4 will struggle to acquire new funds to invest in home loans. There you have it: the business model of the Australian banks breaks. Australians have been fooled to believe that because you need 20% down payment to get a loan from the Big 4, their lending practices are safer than those of banks that offered 0% down payment in low property-cost cities in the U.S.

But here is the big problem that will ultimately arise from a crash in property prices: It will become clear that there are a lot more home loans in Australia where homebuyers have come up with less than 10% and the banks came up with the other 90%+.

Even though I give the Australian banking system the benefit of the doubt in this book and state that 20% is the minimum deposit/collateral a bank demands, that is really not the case—and that is of great concern when the bubble pops. Why? Because a lot of new homebuyers are taking on more than 80% leverage. But even if 20% was the bare minimum deposit required to buy a home, you can see the amount of toxic debt that is in the marketplace. It's not so simple for a bank to sell a foreclosed home. It costs money and time.

In summary, deleveraging events are tough to deal with. Although Australia will fare better than most other countries in the Asia-Pacific region when the China bubble bursts, it will still be very painful. Homes, jobs and hope will be lost for a period of time. But inevitably, one way or another, the economy will bounce back, and our banks will forever be more responsible in their lending habits. New industries will be developed, and the best innovations generally arise during tough times because industries are forced to solve problems that benefit their profitability.

Chapter Twelve

Conclusion

Looking back on these chapters, it is clear that I provide an unpopular view of the Australian economy. I press the hard facts that are very rarely discussed in Australian society. But it is important for any economy and its people to recognize the true state of their economy when certain aspects of it seem to be a bit out of whack. In Australia, the three pillars are the most important industries in the Australian economy. As this book suggests, there is an enormous amount of credit that has fueled the three pillars to a point where it is near impossible for them to be able to absorb any shock to the economic system.

The Big 4 banks have an unsustainable business model. Their flawed strategy to lend more than they did the year before can easily be unraveled, and can easily send these banks into bankruptcy. They are highly leveraged banks that have made enormous bets on just two industries—the second and third pillars of the Australian economy. Because of the high debt ratios that the second and third pillars have within their industries, there is not much room to navigate any shock to the system.

Australian homebuyers are the most exposed to debt of any homebuyers in the Western world. And unless I am gravely mistaken, Australian households have taken on more debt by ratio and sum than households in any other Western country with a population more than 2 million. Let's face it—if the average home loan in the state of NSW is $507,000, households on average are taking on enormous amounts of debt. It is inconceivable for any state in any Western country in the world outside Australia to have an average home loan size this big. Why? Because across the board there are hardly any cities in the world with property prices greater than $500,000. It's that simple. But there are countries, states and cities with a greater median household-income level than those in Australia.

Australia has made one big bet on continuous Chinese growth. This book illustrates that should there be continuous growth in fixed investments in China (particularly in residential real estate), China will inevitably build a new dwelling for every single citizen in China in less than a decade. This doesn't make sense. And I believe the Chinese will inevitably come to their senses. But regardless of what they do to try to cover the economic shortfall of a decrease in construction, there is no other sector of the Chinese economy even close to being able to cover that shortfall. Not even exports.

When the Chinese reduce their demand for Australian iron ore, it will be catastrophic for Australia. The cost to mining companies to extract iron ore from the ground is at least six times more than it was in 2001. The mining companies cannot afford to have the spot price of iron ore sent back to the historical norm. Unfortunately, that is generally what happens when bubbles pop, and today there are so many plausible triggers that could send the spot price of iron ore into a tailspin. Toxic shadow banking credit and overdevelopment in China are the key triggers. And both those triggers are pretty much outside the scope of what the Chinese government can bail out. It is impossible for the Chinese government to control such a large-scale informal lending industry. And there is not much the Chinese government can do to stop changing opinions regarding the over-construction in China. If there has ever been a hugely unmistakable property bubble in the world, this is it. And inevitably it will be the catalyst of a domino effect that takes out the second pillar of the Australian economy.

With the second and third pillar of the Australian economy being so greatly exposed, any impact from a slowdown in Chinese demand of iron ore will flow through to the Australian financial institutions. The Big 4 will find it increasingly difficult to get access to credit when confidence in Australia is low and there are job losses and high currency volatility—which leads to the banks becoming more constrained in regards to their lending capabilities. With the third pillar of the Australian economy being so dependent on toxic-level lending, there is only one way the Australian property market can go—down.

For years, Australian pundits have been telling the world that the Australian property market is "different." But based on the data, it is clear that Australia's property market is in no way different from any other. Property prices have gotten as high as they have because of the banks' willingness to lend excessively. Excessive lending creates the artificial demand that would have not existed otherwise. That is how property bubbles are formed, and that is why they pop. This is what history tells us. Australia is not so different and smart that it has found a way to defy the common laws of economics. So many countries—from Russia to the United States and Japan—have tried to defy the laws of economics in the past and failed. These are three different economies with different cultures and economic models. No matter how different an economy seems, when there is too much debt, credit or direct investment relative to GDP, the economy will inevitably flop.

Pundits in Australia tell us that recourse lending in Australia makes the property market different. They believe that when a homebuyer is fully liable for all the debt, he or she has more incentive to pay off that debt. But when an individual loses a job and cannot pay debts, it doesn't matter whether the loan is recourse or non-recourse. You simply cannot pay your debt! Ask yourself—is this a good enough reason for property prices to remain as high as they are? Unfortunately the answer is a resounding "no." One only has to look at the GFC and what happened in Dubai over that period. Property prices collapsed in Dubai, and if you couldn't pay your home mortgage there, the chance of going to prison was pretty high! That is as good a reason as any to pay off your loan, but many households simply could not find a way. And property prices collapsed. The expats with unserviceable debt fled the UAE, never to return.

The Australian real estate and banking pundits have been very successful in convincing the greater Australian public into believing that the high cost of real estate in Australia is justified. Unfortunately for the pundits, the data on paper presents a completely opposite conclusion. There is clearly no housing shortage in Australia. There is clearly no shortage of land. Fly over Sydney and see how much farmland there is around the outskirts of the city. Melbourne, too! The only reason there are more buyers in the marketplace than there should be is that the banks are willing to lend excessively. Our major cities by density share absolutely no common characteristics to some of the most expensive property markets in the world, but they share similar costs in real estate per square meter. But the pundits, again, have successfully overshadowed the data and convinced homebuyers to pay ridiculous sums of money to buy property.

With the pundits and local bankers successfully convincing Australians that things are "different," Australian households are now more than ever taking on toxic debt in droves. Of course you will never hear a CEO of a Big 4 bank publically state that Australia is in the midst of a housing bubble— the Big 4 are making an absolute fortune by copying the Lehman model. If anyone asked Richard Fuld, the CEO of Lehman Brothers, fifteen months before Lehman Brothers went bust if he had problems sleeping at night because of the amount of risk the bank had taken, he would also have said no. This leaves me to believe that the Big 4 are not in a position to cover their losses when the property bubble bursts. And worst of all, our banks have assets on their balance sheets that are fairly in line with, or greater than, those which Lehman had on its balance sheet a year before it went bust. In addition, the banks in Australia are so big that they each have assets on their balance sheets equivalent to 42% to 49% of GDP. They are too big to fail and technically too big to save by the government.

Lehman's assets were only equivalent to around 5% of the American GDP. When the Australian banking system melts down, one way or another it will cost the Australian government hundreds of billions. That type of money is not easy to find unless you print it. If a country with a $1.5 trillion GDP prints $200 billion or more, the economy is sent into a tailspin and inflation skyrockets to an inconceivable level. Just look at what happened to the $USD versus global currencies when the U.S. kept on printing money. It went to historic lows against a wealth of currencies, including the $AUD. And the U.S.'s problem was only a fraction of what Australia's problem could be if one or more of the Big 4 either gets bailed out or nationalized. Furthermore, I cannot fathom the Australian government bailing out a bank without nationalizing it. The Australia public will not accept it. But just as bad is that Australian individuals are shareholders of the Big 4. It is possible they may find the value of the stocks they have in the banks become worthless. For years to come the taxpayers will be paying for the mistakes of others.

You don't have to be a macroeconomist to see the challenges Australia will face—what you do need to have is a clear and objective view. In Australia, with such vested interest in mining and real estate, there is a clear lack of objectivity. The country doesn't have enough debate on the key challenges that the Australian economy faces. There is no strategy to execute if a domino effect makes its way to Australia's borders. Planning is weak, as is the willingness of Australian leaders from both sides of politics to do something about it. The Rudd and Gillard leadership was simply asleep at the wheel. The RBA has been asleep at the wheel. Both government and the RBA have essentially been in Disneyland. They think they're managing an economy, but essentially they've been managing a credit bubble, and they've been incredibly successful and lucky to date in doing so. Their success can concretely be attributed to the lifeline China threw Australia in 2008 in the form of acquiring every possible ounce of Australian natural resources that could be scraped up from the ground. At that point Australia had the opportunity to face the facts that there was already a credit bubble in Australia, and that it could pop. Yes, it would have possibly left Australia in a mild recession, but the pain wouldn't have been worse than the pain Australia will inevitably witness in the near future when the three bubbling pillars—all with toxic levels of debt—simply pop at the same time by the same cause-effect.

It will only be then that the majority of the Australian public will realize that Australia had a credit-fueled property bubble. Unfortunately, by then it will generally be too late for those holding a significant amount of debt to navigate their ways through rough seas. If Australian property buyers were as cashed up as Australians think they are, the balance sheets of the banks would show a lot fewer assets and less long term-debt. It is clear that many Australians haven't done their research on the true state of the Australian economy.

Today, when an Australian buys a house, he or she should be prepared for a day when the value of the purchased property might be worth half of what it is today. Engaging with that approach will probably make any property purchase a calculated purchase. As long as the property buyer takes this approach, there is a better chance he or she is more prepared to weather a financial storm, and also more prepared to manage liabilities.

Throughout the course of the book I make many comparisons. I think it's pretty clear that the Australian economy would probably be better off and more diverse if property prices had not reached such high prices; to date, only the banks and property owners have profited, while costing the Australian government billions in annual income write-offs. When an industry can profit from capital gain but not from yield, it generally shows that the industry is in a speculative state. That is exactly where the Australian property market is as I'm writing this book. Buyers and the Big 4 have speculated that property prices will only go up. If they didn't believe property prices were going up, they wouldn't invest. There is more confidence in play than logic. Over in Houston, you can get 13% yield on your property investment. That pays off the mortgage, property taxes and still puts money in your pocket. In Australia, this is impossible. Yields are simply too low. On paper, Australians are lousy property investors. Worst of all, they've probably made investment decisions using inaccurate data. And when property makes up roughly 80% of the total asset value of Australia, any drop in prices will be absolutely devastating. If property today, as an asset class, is calculated at $5 trillion, a 20% drop in house prices would equate to $1 trillion in asset depreciation—and a 50% drop would reflect $2.5 trillion in depreciation. That is 1.6x Australia's total GDP. There is no country in the Western world so dependent on property. Unfortunately, when property takes such a large proportion of the asset valuation, it inevitably declines.

As an Australian returning to Australia after living overseas for almost a decade, it is incredible to see how this country has changed from the outside looking in. Australia today is a strong exporting nation, but the economy is very sheltered. What is clear is that Australian investors do not like to venture into unchartered waters. Innovation is very scarce when compared to other Western nations. When the majority of a country's individual investors, financial institution and growth models depend on just a handful of industries, the country as a whole is essentially speculating. Too much money gets pumped into overly large industries that have overly expensive assets. But that's the price a country pays when all bets are on the same industry. I'm pretty sure that if I walked into one of the Big 4 today to ask for financing to build my clean technology company, they would all decline. But with my cash, if I asked them for financing to buy a property, they would all be more than willing to provide me the funding to purchase a property. In addition, if they were actually willing to provide me financing for my clean technology company, they would offer nowhere near the leverage I would get if the financing was intended for a property purchase. What I'm saying is this: if the Australian banks were lending to property investors using the same paradigm of risk as they do when lending to a business outside of the second or third pillars, there would be even distribution of debt across the Australian economy and a lot less exposure overall for the Big 4 to any economic shock.

Sooner than later, Australia will find itself caught up in a position where it doesn't want to be. When the Australian economy either stalls or produces negative growth, it will take a very hard hit. Private sector debt is already too high—way too high for the private sector to borrow its way out of a tough situation. This will cause a significant amount of pain for Australian households. And the many households holding toxic debt will be the most affected. Recession will suck the life out of Pillars Two and Three. As bad as recessions—even depressions—can get, there is always light at the end of the tunnel. Recessions open doors to new innovation, and they force industries to creatively participate more in the solving of industry problems.

I am confident that after the "recession we have to have," Australia will be able to build a more diverse economy that will allow the Australian economy to stimulate the nation's intellect. It will inevitably diversify. Australia as a Western country will become more competitive. Today's Australia cannot compete in the international arena because the cost of doing business in Australia is simply too high. A weakened dollar that has been forced down by the market opens doors. The federal government will see value in Australia having a weaker currency, affordable housing and, more importantly, diversity. In this instance, history supports this type of economic model and strategy.

Australia welcomes foreign investment. While a deleveraging event will be a devastating experience for Australians to go through, a weaker currency and a lower level of private sector debt will create the ultimate formula to attract foreign investment across the greater spectrum of the Australian economy. This is invaluable. Affordable investment into a Western nation is what many multinational corporations seek, and Australia does have a fairly attractive corporate tax regime for foreign investors. Nobody likes to invest into a country when its currency is overvalued. But when a currency is at its historic norm, money can simply pour into a country more evenly and can impact the greater population and industries rather than just the mining and real estate industries. And Australian entrepreneurs and businesses improve their profitability by having lower fixed costs related to rent and raw materials. Steel, copper and other metals are today extraordinarily expensive by historic measures. The cost of these goods are simply extracting too much of the overall cost of construction and manufacturing. When China stops building, Australia has a golden opportunity to use the excess stockpiles of iron ore to build new infrastructure at a much cheaper cost than it would cost to build today. Recessions are bad, but they open doors to the possibility of doing things that would have otherwise been simply unaffordable in good times. I truly hope Australia does exploit this in the midst of economic pain.

I am sincere in my hope that this commentary has provided a more complete and well-rounded understanding of the current state of the Australian economy, and clarity about where it will probably end up. The road ahead is definitely a rocky one for the Australian economy—it is always important to realize that in good times, one should always prepare for the worst.

Notes and Sources:

Introduction

Australian GDP Data: Tradingeconomics.com and Australian Bureau of Statistics (ABS)

Chapter 1

FDI attractiveness: IMD World Competitiveness Center and comparisons of tax and investment advantages on various national tax office websites, including ATO.gov.au and Austrade.gov.au

Miner wages: Based on various discussions with in-the-field employees from various mining companies and locations.

Money Pouring into Australia: Based on data from the ABS and various comments by Wayne Swan.

Unemployment rate: Tradingeconomics.com and ABS

Trade Data: Austrade.gov.au

Historical Interest Rate Data: tradingeconomics.com, ABS and loansense.com.au

Public Sector Debt Data: Tradingeconomics.com

Minimum Salary: Australian Bureau of Statistics (ABS) & Australian Fair Work Ombudsman

Chapter 2

Population Densities: Based on data from Wikipedia.

Income in Vaud: Swiss Statistics

UHNW Data: World City Millionaire Rankings; Wealth Insight; May 2013 & New York City Home to 70 Billionaires, the most in the world: New York Daily News May 9, 2013

Houston Population Growth Data: City of Houston Website

The Woodlands Texas Household Income Data: City-data.com

Most Expensive Cities Rankings: World Most Expensive Real Estate Marjets: CNBC March 2013

City GDP and Population Data: The Brookings Institute and Wikipedia.

House Price Data and Income Data: Demographia 10th Annual International Housing Affordability Survey: 2014. 3rd Quarter 2013; Alan Bertaud

Property Tax Information: Personal knowledge through time spent in the discussed cities.

Cost of business trips to various cities: Concur Expense IQ Report 2013.

Chapter 3

Sydney Morning herald Quotes:

"Sydney property boom drives prices up by $100,000." Toby Johnstone, January 30, 2014. www.smh.com.au

"Record-breaking Sydney auction market to end (year) on a high." Andrew Wilson, December 20, 2013. www.smh.com.au

"Auction fever spreads to top-end property." Lucy Macken, February 15, 2014 www.smh.com.au

"Busiest February for auctions on record as owners rush to sell." Toby Johnstone, February 15, 2014. www.smh.com.au

"Records smashed on Sydney's famous laneway." and "Unrenovated one-bedder on 51 sq m fetches $745,000 as clearance rate hits 84.4 percent." Stephen Nicholls, February 8, 2014. www.smh.com.au

Auction Clearance Result Data: APM Property Monitors & Domain Property February 22, 2104

"Boom time as average home loan crosses $500,000.' Anthony Lawes, September 4, 2013. www.smh.com.au

Mining Stock declines in 2008: Google Finance & Yahoo Finance

Australian Fundamentals: Speech by Wayne Swan at IMF 2012 Annual Meeting; Tokyo

Chapter 4

Financial & Balance Sheet Data

CBA: Financial statements from 2009-2013 & Yahoo Finance & Google Finance

WBC: Financial statements from 2009-2013 & Yahoo Finance & Google Finance

ANZ: Financial statements from 2009-2013 & Yahoo Finance & Google Finance

NAB: Financial statements from 2009-2013 & Yahoo Finance & Google Finance

Lehman Brothers: Financial Statements from 2006-2008

Zurich Cantonal Bank: Financial Statements from 20012-2013

Breakdown of Australian Private Sector Debt: Australian Debt Clock
http://www.australiandebtclock.com.au

Household count: Australian Census Bureau. 2011 data used.

"CBA chief Ian Narev not losing sleeping over property bubble fears." Clancy Yeates, August 12, 2013. www.smh.com.au

Ian Narev Quote: "'The reasons we don't think we have a housing bubble is not just because a lot of the incidences of price rises are quite location specific, but also if you look at the fundamental dynamics of supply and demand, the current levels of prices are well supported by levels of supply and demand," Ian Narev quote from Australian Banking and Finance www.australianbankingandfinance.com

Chapter 5

Gough, Niel & Barboza, David. "Credit Tightens in China as Central Bank Takes a Hard Line." New York Times, June 20, 2013.

China's Real Estate Bubble; 60 Minutes; CBS
http://www.cbsnews.com/video/watch/?id=50142079n

Residential Construction Data: China National Bureau of Statistics

Average Dwelling Size in China: "How Big is a House? Average House Size by Country", Lindsay Wilson, July 17, 2013. www.reneweconomy.com.au

China GDP Data: From several sources including Official Chinese Govt. Data, World Bank, Trading Economics and Wikipedia.

Visual Change in China: Based on my numerous trips to China and discussions with locals, industry professionals and local entrepreneurs.

Fixed Investment Data: Based on several sources including the IMF and CIA World Factbook.

Chapter 6

Rio Tinto: Financial Statements from 2001-13

BHP: Financial Statements from 2008-2013

Fortescue Metals: Financial Statements from 2011-2013

Google Finance and Yahoo Finance for chart graphs.

$AUD: Based on historic $AUD charts on www.cnbc.com, www.xe.com *and Yahoo finance.*

Mining Growth Forecasts: Based on annual reports of several mining companies including BHP, Rio Tinto and Fortescue Metals.

Chapter 7

"Apartment sells for $1.235 million above reserve."
Stephen Nicholls, February 22, 2014.
www.news.domain.com.au

Joe Hockey quotes based on interview on CNBC USA:
October 14, 2013. Interview by Amanda Drury.

Australian Dwelling Sizes: Demographia 10th Annual
International Housing Affordability Survey: 2014. 3rd
Quarter 2013; Alan Bertaud

Harry Dent and Dr Wilson. "Property Prices will
Plummet Says Specialist." February 16, 2014: Kim
Arlington: www.smh.com.au

Property Valuations: Demographia 10th Annual
International Housing Affordability Survey: 2014. 3rd
Quarter 2013; Alan Bertaud

Occupied vs. Unoccupied Dwellings: Australian
Census Bureau. 2011 data.

Rules for Foreign Property Buyers: Laws are written
clearly on the Australian Foreign Investment Review
Board website.

Foreign Buyers buy 12.5% of New Homes: "Aussie
Rules for Overseas Buyers Won't Solve London's
Housing Bubble." February 5, 2014, Margaret
McKenzie; www.theconversation.com

Number of Las Vegas Real Estate Agents: Nevada
Division of Real Estate & "This year's top lowest
ranked professions." November 13, 2013. Linda
Strasberg. www.examiner.com

Auctions: Based on my attendance of multiple auctions.

Investment calculations based on government stamp duty calculators and estimated council rates based on similar properties versus the hypothetical properties discussed.

Property Affordability Classifications: Demographia 10th Annual International Housing Affordability Survey: 2014. 3rd Quarter 2013; Alan Bertaud

Chapter 8

Australian Economic Data: Trading Economics & Australian Bureau of Statistics.

Interest Rates, Private & Public Sector Debt Data: Trading Economics.

Public Sector Debt Year-on-year: Australian Bureau of Statistics & Reserve Bank of Australia.

Wayne Swan Comments: CNBC interview with Wayne Swan on Capital Connection, July 11, 2012. www.cnbc.com

Chapter 9 and 10

Hypothetical scenarios are hypothetical instances that have not come to fruition. Data is used from previous sources mentioned above to guide the storylines.

Chapter 11 and Conclusion

Previously used data and findings reflect the storyline and personal commentary to end the book on a good note.

Book Cover Design By Xtock/Shutterstock.com

Disclaimer

The views and commentaries expressed on these pages reflect my personal views and opinion in my individual capacity. Any statements made in this book about persons or groups are only personal opinions and are not intended to be truthful factual representations nor disparagements of these persons or groups. In addition, please be duly informed that when comments are made about a past or present government policy, issue, or historical event, I am only relying on the publicly available facts and I have no personal knowledge of the facts or the merits of the issues on which I comment outside of what has been publicly published. I try my very best to understand the facts and other matters that I comment on, yet I would still strongly recommend that you should read these opinions and other sources again and judge them by yourself.

Regards

Lindsay David

www.ingramcontent.com/pod-product-compliance
Lightning Source LLC
Chambersburg PA
CBHW051641170526
45167CB00001B/283